S0-AOM-183

50¢

ESSENTIAL TRUTH:

INVITING CHRIST INTO MY REALITY

Connect with God. Connect with others.
Connect with life.

Essential Truth Youth Edition: Inviting Christ into My Reality
Leader Book
© 2005 Serendipity

Published by Serendipity House Publishers
Nashville, Tennessee

ISBN: 1-5749-4242-5

Dewey Decimal Classification: 230
Subject Headings:
GOD \ CHRISTIAN LIFE \ YOUTH--RELIGIOUS LIFE

Unless otherwise indicated, all Scripture quotations are taken from the
Holman Christian Standard Bible®. Copyright © 1999, 2000, 2002, 2003 by Holman Bible Publishers.
Used by permission.

Scriptures marked NIV are taken from the *Holy Bible, New International Version*, Copyright © 1973,
1978, 1984 by International Bible Society. Used by permission.

To purchase additional copies of this resource or other studies:
ORDER ONLINE at www.SerendipityHouse.com
WRITE Serendipity House, 117 10th Avenue North, Nashville, TN 37234
FAX (615) 277-8181
PHONE (800) 525-9563

1-800-525-9563
www.SerendipityHouse.com

Printed in the United States of America
11 10 09 08 07 06 05   1 2 3 4 5 6 7 8 9 10

CONTENTS

SESSION 1
Who is God ... Really?   9

SESSION 2
Undone: How Do We Respond to God?   21

SESSION 3
Love God, Love People: What Does God Expect of Us?   35

SESSION 4
Some Old Book: Why Does the Bible Matter?   47

SESSION 5
Jesus: Prophet, Priest, King, or Homeboy?   61

SESSION 6
Breaking the Bond: Can I Be Free?   73

SESSION 7
Fear Factor: What Happens When Someone Dies?   85

SESSION 8
Get Connected: Why Do I Need Other Christians?   99

SESSION 9
Vintage Faith: How Do I Keep It Real?   111

SESSION 10
Life in Sin City: How Do I Resist Temptation?   123

SESSION 11
The Great Paradox: What Matters in Life?   137

SESSION 12
May the Force Be With You: What's Up With the Holy Spirit?   149

SESSION 13
Amazing: What's So Important About Grace?   163

Acknowledgments   174
GROUP DIRECTORY   176

EXPERIENCE

Combine *teaching that engages a large-group* with dynamic *small-group experiences and discussions* and the result is students grappling with reality and real life change. Throughout 13 sessions, small-groups will find power in just being together in community. Help them connect with God ... connect with each other ... connect with life! Each session consists of a four-part agenda. In addition, "Get Ready" and Now What?" segments enable students to dig a little deeper and give God more opportunity to impact their lives.

 ### Get Ready

To get the most from this experience, students should spend time with God each day leading up to your session. They simply wrap their brains around the short Bible passages, listen to God, and jot down thoughts and insights.

 ### So What?

The master-teacher will lead the entire group in understanding what God has to say on the topic. Content has biblical depth, yet is engaging. Students can follow along, jot notes, and respond to questions in their Student Books.

 ### LifePoint

Welcome and communicate the "LifePoint" or big idea for the session, and then divide students into small groups. NOTE: If feasible, keep the same groups together each week to enhance the depth of group dynamic and potential for life change.

 ### Do What?

All study should direct us toward action and life change. The goal in small groups is to be real with each other in order to connect with God, with others, and with life. Students will find power to integrate truth into life with the support and prayers of other students.

 ### Say What?

Small-group facilitators lead students in interactive experiences and discussions. "Random Question of the Week" will open students up and encourage them to join activities or discussions that lead into the session topic.

 ### Now What?

To see real power in life, encourage students not to just leave the session and go on with life as normal. The "Now What?" assignments help them continue their journeys and give them opportunity to go deeper with God.

AT A GLANCE

Daily time with God
& your journal

Get Ready

LifePoint

Large Group:
welcome & theme

Say What?

Small Group:
fun & interaction

So What?

Large Group:
teaching & discovery
(Master Teacher)

Do What?

Small Group:
Getting real
& connecting

Continue your journey...

now What?

LEADERS AND FACILITATORS

Every Life Connections group must fill three important roles. Each responsibility is vital to the success of the class.

Teacher — The teacher is the key leader of any Life Connections group.
It is the responsibility of the teacher to:
1. enlist facilitators and apprentices.
2. make facilitators and apprentices aware of their roles and be certain these responsibilities are carried out.
3. meet periodically with facilitators to train, encourage, and inspire them.
4. cast vision for and keep the group focused on the goals of the group.
5. guide group members to understand and commit to the group covenant.
6. be sure the group utilizes, fills, and evangelizes through use of the empty chair concept.
7. act as the Master Teacher for the group.
8. keep the group on task throughout each session.

Facilitator — Each subgroup will have a facilitator. It is the responsibility of the facilitators to:
1. lead each individual in their subgroup to participate in "Say What?" activities.
2. guide those in their subgroup to commit to apply the lessons learned in the "Do What?" section of the weekly session.
3. with sensitivity and wisdom lead their subgroup to support one another during the "Do What?" closing and involve their subgroup in ministry and evangelism.
4. encourage students to go deeper by completing the "Get Ready" and "Now What?" times on their own between sessions.
5. minister to the needs of their subgroup members and lead them to minister to the needs of one another both during and between meetings.

Apprentice — Every subgroup must have an apprentice. When the group consistently has eight or more in attendance, the group should divide into two groups. The apprentice will become the facilitator of the new group and choose an apprentice who will someday be the facilitator of a group. It is the role of the apprentice to:
1. learn from the facilitator of their group.
2. make welcome all new subgroup members.
3. be certain **Student Books** and pens or pencils, and other supplies are available for all students.
4. turn in prayer requests.
5. encourage participation by actively participating themselves.
6. lead the group when the facilitator is unavailable.

For more information and frequently asked questions about Life Connections, visit our Web site at *www.SerendipityHouse.com.*

CORE VALUES

Community:
God is relational, so He created us to live in relationship with Him and each other. Authentic community involves sharing life together and connecting on many levels with the people in our group.

Group Process:
Developing authentic community requires a step-by-step process. It's a journey of sharing our stories with each other and learning together.

Interactive Bible Study:
God provided the Bible as an instruction manual of life. We need to deepen our understanding of God's Word. People learn and remember more as they wrestle with truth and learn from others. The process of Bible discovery and group interaction will enhance our growth.

Experiential Growth:
The goal of studying the Bible together is not merely a quest for knowledge; this should result in real life change. Beyond solely reading, studying, and dissecting the Bible, being a disciple of Christ involves reunifying knowledge with experience. We do this by bringing our questions to God, opening a dialogue with our hearts (instead of killing our desires), and utilizing other ways to listen to God speak to us (group interaction, nature, art, movies, circumstances, etc.). Experiential growth is always grounded in the Bible as God's primary means of revelation and our ulti-mate truth-source.

The Power of God:
Our processes and strategies will be ineffective unless we invite and embrace God's presence and power. In order to experience community and growth, Jesus must the centerpiece of our group experiences and the Holy Spirit must be at work.

Redemptive Community:
Healing best happens within the context of community and in relationship. A key aspect of our spiritual development is seeing ourselves through the eyes of others, sharing our stories, and ultimately being set free from the secrets and the lies we embrace that enslave our souls.

Mission:
God has invited us into a larger story with a great mission. It is a mission that involves setting captives free and healing the broken-hearted (Isaiah 61:1-2). However, we can only join in this mission to the degree that we've let Jesus bind up our wounds and set us free. As a group experiences true redemptive commu-nity, other people will be attracted to that group, and through that group to Jesus. We should be alert to inviting others while we maintain (and continue to fill) an "empty chair" in our meetings to remind us of others who need to encounter God and authentic Christian community.

GROUP COVENANT

It is important that your group covenant together, agreeing to live out important group values. Once these values are agreed upon, your group will be on its way to experiencing true Christian community. It's very important that your group discuss these values—preferably as you begin this study. The first session would be most appropriate. (Check the rules to which each member of your group agrees.)

☐ Priority: While you are in this course of study, you give the group meetings priority.

☐ Participation: Everyone is encouraged to participate and no one dominates.

☐ Respect: Everyone is given the right to his or her own opinion, and all questions are encouraged and respected.

☐ Confidentiality: Anything that is said in the meeting is never repeated outside the meeting without permission. *Note: Church staff may be required by law to report illegal activities.*

☐ Life Change: We will regularly assess our own progress in applying *LifePoints* and encourage one another in our pursuit of becoming more like Christ.

☐ Care and Support: Permission is given to call upon each other at any time, especially in times of crisis. The group will provide care for every member.

☐ Accountability: We agree to let the members of the group hold us accountable to the commitments we make in whatever loving ways we decide upon. Unsolicited advice giving is not permitted.

☐ Empty Chair: The group is open to welcoming new people at every meeting.

☐ Mission: We agree as a group to reach out and invite others to join us.

☐ Ministry: We will encourage one another to volunteer and serve in a ministry and to support missions by giving financially and/or personally serving.

Session

1

WHO IS GOD...REALLY?

Connections Prep

MAIN LIFEPOINT: God is not some concept invented by smart guys in a research lab; He is beyond description or definition. He is the great "I AM" who is personal and spiritual, yet totally awesome and above us.

To reinforce the LifePoint, leaders and small-group facilitators should understand the following more detailed CheckPoints and "Do" Points.

BIBLE STUDY CHECKPOINTS:
- Examine the ways people view God
- Understand what the Bible says about who God really is
- Evaluate how the reality of God affects every aspect of our lives

LIFE CHANGE "DO" POINTS:
- Accept who God is, not who we think He is
- Commit to study the Bible consistently to discover who God is
- Connect with God daily through prayer and quiet times that focus our attention on Him

PREPARATION:
- ☐ Review the *Leader's Book* for this session and prepare your teaching.
- ☐ Set up the TV/DVD or video system.
- ☐ Determine how you will subdivide students into small discussion groups.
- ☐ Recruit mature students or adults as small-group facilitators. Be sure these facilitators plan to attend.

REQUIRED SUPPLIES:
- ☐ *Essential Truth: Inviting Christ into My Reality* Leader books for each group facilitator
- ☐ *Essential Truth: Inviting Christ into My Reality* Student books for each student
- ☐ Pens or pencils for each student
- ☐ A copy of the movie *The Prince of Egypt* by Dreamworks
- ☐ TV/DVD or video system
- ☐ 1 cup of Mountain Dew® for each small group
- ☐ 1 cup of Mountain Lightning or other generic version of Dew
- ☐ 1 cup of Lemonade for each small group
- ☐ 1 cup of Vinegar for each small group

Get Ready

Read one these short Bible passages each day, and spend a few minutes wrapping your brain around it. Be sure to jot down any insights you discover.

MONDAY

Read Exodus 3:1-3

God got Moses' attention through an unusual sight—a bush that was on fire but was not being consumed. What's the strangest thing that has happened to you recently? Have you ever felt that God was trying to get your attention through this event or another one?

TUESDAY

Read Exodus 3:4-6

Who is the most important person you have ever met? Were you intimidated to be around this person? Why was Moses afraid when God spoke to him?

WEDNESDAY

Read Exodus 3:7-10

Do you think that God knows about your struggles? How does this passage give you hope? Try to imagine the emotions that Moses experienced during this moment.

THURSDAY

Read Exodus 3:11-12

Often people feel unworthy or unprepared for major life opportunities. What is God's response to Moses' question, "Who am I?" How do you think God would respond if you asked the same question?

FRIDAY

Read Exodus 3:13-15

Why are names important? How did you get your name? Why do you think Moses wants to be able to give the Israelites a name for God?

SATURDAY

Read Exodus 3:1-15

Read over the entire story. Can you relate to Moses' journey in any specific ways? What themes do you see in this story that are a part of your experience?

SUNDAY

Read Hebrews 11:23-28

Why should Moses be included in the "Faith Hall of Fame"? How did the experience of the burning bush prepare Moses for the purpose God called him to?

LARGE-GROUP OPENING:
Get everyone's attention. Make announcements. Open your session with a prayer. Read the LifePoint to the students.

 LifePoint

God is not some concept invented by smart guys in a research lab; He is beyond description or definition. He is the great "I AM" who is personal and spiritual, yet totally awesome and above us.

SMALL-GROUP TIME:
Instruct students to separate into smaller groups of 4-8, preferably in a circle configuration. Call on the mature student or adult leaders you recruited to facilitate each small group through this "Say What?" segment.

 # Say What? *(15 MINUTES)*

Random Question of the Week:
Why does cottage cheese have an expiration date?

Group Experience: The Real Thing

Set up a blind taste test using at least two variations of a popular soft drink. For fun, you could do it like this:

- Cup One: Mountain Lighting (or any generic version of Dew)
- Cup Two: Lemonade
- Cup Three: Mountain Dew
- Cup Four: Vinegar

Blindfold at least four students, and tell them that you are doing a blind taste test for a major soft drink company. There are four variations of the new drink being considered. One is the "regular" version, which, if chosen, will be labeled as "classic." The students' job is to decide which tastes best. Place all four cups in front of the students and instruct them to drink one at a time on your cue. Tell them that the "audience" is going to help them decide by their reaction which version is best. Be sure to have some paper towels and trash cans handy as they "react" to the last cup!

After the taste test, discuss the following questions:

1. In the taste test, only one drink was the real thing. In our world, there are many different kinds of gods, but only one is the real thing. Can you name some examples of gods (past or present) that people have followed?

2. The original soft drink has some unique qualities that make it distinctive. What are some characteristics of God that make Him distinctive as well?

3. Perhaps someone preferred one of the variations to the real soft drink. How can you and I be sure that the God we are following is the right one if some people prefer another version of god?

LARGE-GROUP TIME: Have the students turn to face the front for this teaching time. Be sure you can make eye contact with each student in the room. Encourage students to follow along and take notes in their *Student Books*.

 # So What? *(30 MINUTES)*

Teaching Outline

I. What people believe about God
A. Polls show vast majority believe in God
B. Deism – God is responsible for creation but does not intervene
C. Pantheism – the universe itself is god
D. New Age – god is in each of us and we can attain divinity

II. God is present
A. He cannot be contained by anything, even time or space
B. He is bigger than the universe, yet closer than our own breath

III. God is holy
A. God is perfect; we're not
B. God's holy perfection can't be in the presence of our failures & sins
C. We should fear God in the sense of awe of His holiness
D. God loves us so much He made a way to reconnect with us through Jesus

IV. God is mystery
A. He's beyond our understanding, but He still reveals Himself to us
B. His name YHWH is the closest sound to breathing
C. Out of respect, ancient Hebrews wouldn't write or speak God's name
D. Yahweh/YHWH means "I AM" – essentially "I am the God who really IS"

V. God is power
A. He's in control and carrying out His plan of rescuing, healing, & redeeming us
B. We have a part to play in God's mission

VI. God is love
A. He won't leave us in a predicament we can't escape
B. God sent Jesus to deliver us because of His awesome love

Share the "So What?" teaching with your students. You may modify it to meet your needs.

Be sure to highlight the underlined information, which gives answers to the *Student Book* questions and fill-in-the-blanks (shown in your margins).

**TEACHING FOR THE
LARGE GROUP**

What People Believe About God

Who or what is God? Since the beginning of recorded history, man has tried to find a way to explain a reason for our existence. Every culture in every era has devised some kind of god to make sense of it all. But what if God isn't what we make Him? What if God isn't someone we find, but someone who finds us? Today we're going to begin to answer some important questions: Who is God ... really? How can we know Him? How can we be sure that my "version" of Him is right and not a figment of my imagination?"

❶ **Poll show that a vast majority of people believe in *God*.**

❷ **Deism teaches that god is responsible for *creation* but generally does not *intervene* in what happens in the world.**

❸ **Pantheism teaches that the *universe* itself is *God* (including all of nature).**

❹ **New Age movements teach that god is in *each* of *us* in the form a heavenly spark that we must get in touch with to discover the *divine*.**

Polls show that ❶ <u>a vast majority of people believe in God</u>. People are interested, but whom are they interested in? What do people mean when they say they believe in "God?" Here are a few variations:

❷ <u>Deism</u> teaches that god is responsible for <u>creation</u> but generally does not <u>intervene</u> in what happens in the world.

❸ <u>Pantheism</u> teaches that the <u>universe</u> itself is <u>God</u> (including all of nature). Carl Sagan, an astronomer, writes, "The idea that God is an oversized white male with a huge flowing beard who sits in the sky and tallies the fall of every sparrow is ludicrous. But if by 'God' one means the set of physical laws that govern the universe, then clearly there is such a God."

❹ <u>New Age movements</u> teach that god is in <u>each of us</u> in the form a heavenly spark that we must get in touch with to discover the <u>divine</u>.

So, how do we define God? Where do we even begin? The Christian God revealed in the Bible is the one we'll examine today. The Bible reveals characteristics of God through stories of His encounters with people. Today we'll look at the story of Moses – a man who asked the same question, "Who is God?"

Learning from the Bible

Learning from
the Bible ...

Exodus 3:1-15

Ask for three
volunteers to come
to the front and read
the parts of (1) the
narrator, (2) Moses,
and (3) God.

[NARRATOR] ¹ *Moses was shepherding the flock of his father-in-law Jethro, the priest of Midian. He led the flock to the far side of the wilderness and came to Horeb, the mountain of God.* ² *Then the Angel of the Lord appeared to him in a flame of fire within a bush. As Moses looked, he saw that the bush was on fire but was not consumed.*
³ *So Moses thought:*
[MOSES] I must go over and look at this remarkable sight. Why isn't the bush burning up?
[NARRATOR] ⁴ *When the Lord saw that he had gone over to look, God called out to him from the bush,*

14

[GOD] "Moses, Moses!"

[MOSES] "Here I am ..."

[GOD] 5 "Do not come closer"... "Take your sandals off your feet, for the place where you are standing is holy ground." ... "I am the God of your father, the God of Abraham, the God of Isaac, and the God of Jacob."

[NARRATOR] Moses hid his face because he was afraid to look at God.

[NARRATOR] 7 Then the Lord said,

[GOD] "I have observed the misery of My people in Egypt, and have heard them crying out because of their oppressors, and I know about their sufferings. 8 I have come down to rescue them from the power of the Egyptians and to bring them from that land to a good and milk and honey.... 9 The Israelites' cry for help has come to Me, and I have also seen the way the Egyptians are oppressing them. 10 Therefore, go. I am sending you to Pharaoh so that you may lead My people, the Israelites, out of Egypt."

[NARRATOR] 11 But Moses asked God,

[MOSES] "Who am I that I should go to Pharaoh and that I should bring the Israelites out of Egypt?"

[GOD] 12 "I will certainly be with you, and this will be the sign to you that I have sent you: when you bring the people out of Egypt, you will all worship God at this mountain."

[NARRATOR] 13 Then Moses asked God,

[MOSES] "If I go to the Israelites and say to them: The God of your fathers has sent me to you, and they ask me, 'What is His name?' what should I tell them?"

[NARRATOR] 14 God replied to Moses,

[GOD] "I AM WHO I AM. This is what you are to say to the Israelites: I AM has sent me to you." 15 God also said to Moses, "Say this to the Israelites: Yahweh, the God of your fathers, the God of Abraham, the God of Isaac, and the God of Jacob, has sent me to you. This is My name forever; this is how I am to be remembered in every generation.

The classic story of Moses and the burning bush reveals timeless truths about the character and person of God. It presents an accurate picture of who God is, what He's up to, and why He cares about us.

We discover at least five aspects of God's character in this story of Moses and the burning bush:

(1) God is Present

God is everywhere (omnipresent) and knows everything (omniscient), yet we can experience Him personally and intensely in our lives. Psalm 139:7-10 (NIV) gives David's experience with this reality: *"Where can I go from your Spirit, where can I flee from your presence? If I go up to the heavens, you are there; if I make my bed in the depths, you are there. If I rise on the wings of the dawn, if I settle on the far side of the sea, even there your hand will guide me, your right hand will hold me*

LARGE-GROUP TIME CONTINUED:
This is the meat of the teaching time. Remind students to follow along and take notes in their *Student Books.*

As you share the "So What?" information with students, make it your own. Use your natural teaching style.

Emphasize underlined information, which gives key points, answers to the *Student Book* questions or fill-in-the-blanks in the (shown in your margins).

GOD IS PRESENT
5 How can God be near to each one of us at the same time?

fast." Jesus explained that, *"God is Spirit"* (John 4:24). **5** He cannot be contained by anything, even space and time! So, God is always with us and always near. He is bigger than the universe and closer than our own breath at the same time.

Does your brain hurt yet? It should! Let's face it — we don't want a God we can figure out with our human minds. That wouldn't be a very big God! We long to know (and our instincts tell us) that there is someone far greater than us who's worthy of devotion, sacrifice, and worship! In this story, Moses meets a God who is real and present.

(2) God is Holy

God is perfect ... "holy." He doesn't make mistakes, is never unsure of His plan, and doesn't change His mind. Since He is holy, He can't be in the presence of wrong attitudes and behaviors (sin). So, why would a perfect being care about people who are fail, are imperfect, and turn from Him? This is one of the great questions of all time! The Bible tells us over and over again that God does care about us! But there are certain realities that cannot be ignored. One is that there's a distance between God and us that's caused by our rebellion or turning away from God and His commands.

GOD IS HOLY
6 What reaction do we see over and over in the Bible when people experience the glory and presence of God?

In the story, God warns Moses to take off his shoes as a sign of respect because he is standing on ground made "holy" by the presence of God. **6** Throughout the Bible, people's response to the presence of God is not what you might think. Most of us think it would be cool to see God in His glory, but those in the Bible who caught a glimpse of God's glory responded with fear. Moses hides his face, Elijah hides in a cave, Isaiah says, "Woe is me!" and shepherds in Bethlehem fall face down. Yet, despite God's perfection, He still loves us and provides a solution to the rebellion and failures that separates us. The Father sent His Son, Jesus Christ, as the bridge to span the gap between us and makes a relationship between unholy people and a holy God possible (reference John 3:16-17).

(3) God is Mystery

God is mysterious and can't be defined. He tells us Himself, "My thoughts are not your Thoughts, and your ways are not My ways" (Isaiah 55:8). Yet, our finite minds need a place to begin. You can imagine how uncomfortable Moses was in his situation. God tells him to do something important, and Moses is concerned about how to convince the people that it really is God speaking to him and not just a bad case of indigestion or delusional thought. Think about it — how would you convince your friends that God showed up in a bush that was on fire while you were walking your dog? When Moses asks, "What should I tell them?" God responds, "I am Yahweh," which in Hebrew means, "to be."

There are several amazing mysteries about this name. First, Hebrew scholars think the letters ❼ "YHWH" (the way God's name is spelled in Hebrew) are phonetically the closest to the sound of breathing. In other words, with every breath we take we affirm God's existence! Pretty cool! Second, ❼ the name was considered so sacred that ancient Hebrews refused to write it or say it in everyday life; they would leave a blank space when they wrote it or a holy pause when they read it. This demonstrates the tremendous respect that this early group of God-followers had for Him. Finally, ❼ we can understand the name of Yahweh or "I AM "as saying, "I am the God who really IS in contrast to other gods that exist only in people's imaginations. This amazing God who revealed himself to Moses still reveals Himself to us today. Remember, the Bible is not the record of our search for God ... it's the record of God's search for us (Genesis 3:10)!

(4) God is Power

❽ God is in control and is carrying out His plan of rescuing, healing, and redeeming us. Yet, God chooses to give choices, opportunities, and responsibilities to us. In Exodus 3:12, God assures Moses that he will succeed chiefly because God is with him. God continues the story He begins here throughout the Old Testament as He "rescues" the nation of Israel time and time again. In the New Testament, God rescues His people once and for all through the Jesus and His saving work. Remember, just because God is in control of the plan doesn't mean that we don't have anything to do. Just as God sent Moses to free the people of Israel from slavery in a foreign land, Jesus sends us, his followers, to join Him in freeing people from bondage to sin. Isn't it amazing that God saves us and then allows us to be a part of His plan to rescue the world?

(5) God is Love

God refuses to leave us stuck in a predicament that we can't escape from. Over and over in the Bible, God tells and shows He cares about the hurting, the captives, and the brokenhearted. In Exodus 3:7, God sees the misery of His people and hears their cries for help. ❾ In this story, God sends Moses to deliver the people from suffering. In the same way, Jesus identified with our suffering and came to deliver us. God understands our hard times (Hebrews 2:18). By dying on the cross, Jesus delivered us from the greatest suffering: the power of death (1 Corinthians 15:54-57) and demonstrated that His nature truly is love (1 John 4:8).

LARGE GROUP:
Show the "Burning Bush" segment from the movie *The Prince of Egypt* movie by DreamWorks.

SMALL-GROUP TIME:
Use this time to help students begin to integrate the truth they've learned into their lives while they connect with the other students in the group, the leaders, and with God.

AFTER THE CLIP:
Ask students to divide back into small groups and discuss the "Do What?" questions. Small-group facilitators should lead the discussions and set the model for being open and honest in responding to questions.

 # Do What? *(15 MINUTES)*

Group Experience: Burning Bush

1. What stood out to you the most about the clip we just saw? Explain.

2. Do you feel you have a better idea of who God is? What has become clearer and what are you still struggling with?

3. Which of the aspects we discovered in Moses' story is the most relevant to your current situation in life?
   - ☐ God's Presence (verses 4-5) – I need to feel God's presence where I am right now.
   - ☐ God's Holiness (verse 5) – I'm dealing with some temptations, failures, or bad choices in my life right now; I need to be closer to God.
   - ☐ God's Love (verses 7-10) – I'm hurting, and I need to be reminded that He cares about me.
   - ☐ God's Power (verse 12) – I need circumstances in my life to change; I need to be reminded that God my rescuer.
   - ☐ God's Mystery (verses 14-15) – I want a God who is bigger than I can understand; I've been tempted to make up a god in my own image who is far too small.

4. What "Egypt" (predicament) would you like God to deliver you from right now?
   - ☐ Painful memories from the past
   - ☐ A bad relationship
   - ☐ Difficulty getting along with parents
   - ☐ Fear or anxiety issues
   - ☐ Uncertainty about my future
   - ☐ Loneliness and/or depression
   - ☐ An attitude or addiction that holds me captive
   - ☐ Other: _____

Small-group facilitators should reinforce the LifePoint for this session, make sure that student's questions are invited and addressed honestly.

 # LifePoint Review

God is not some concept invented by smart guys in a research lab;He is beyond description or definition. He is the great "I AM" who is personal and spiritual, yet totally awesome and above us.

"Do" Points:

These "Do" Points will help you grab hold of this week's LifePoint. Be open and honest as answer the questions within your small group.

1. <u>Accept who God is, not who you think He is.</u> It's easy to try to create a god we can manage. Determine today to discover who He truly is.
   Why might it be difficult to pursue and accept new ideas about God?

2. <u>Commit to study the Bible consistently.</u> If the Bible is where we'll discover who God is, then we need to get as much of it into our lives as we can.
   What steps do you need to take to commit to regular Bible reading and study?

3. <u>Connect with God daily through prayer and quiet times that focus your attention on Him.</u> Spiritual life is not just a little compartment of our lives. Our relationship with God is so much richer if we maintain an ongoing, daily conversation with Him. **Have you ever had a good time of connection with God? Tell the group about it.**

Prayer Connection:

Be sure to end your session by asking students to share prayer needs with one another, especially as they relate to issues brought up by today's session.

This is the time to encourage, support, and pray for each other in our journeys to grasp who God really is and how much He cares for each of us.

Share prayer needs with the group, especially those related to knowing and connecting with God. Your group facilitator will close your time in prayer.

Encourage students to list prayer needs for others in their books so they can pray for one another during the week. Assign a student coordinator in each small group to gather the group's requests and e-mail them to the group members.

Prayer Needs:

ɳσω Whaʈ?

Deepen your understanding of who God is, and continue the journey you've begun today by choosing one of the following assignments to complete this week:

Option #1:

Research what different religious systems teach about God and Jesus. Some major belief systems include: Judaism, Christianity, Islam, Hinduism, and Buddhism (add more if you like). What is the main difference between the Christian God and the belief system(s) you dig into? Record what you find in a journal.

Option #2:

Find all the different names given to God in the Bible (A concordance or the information in the back of your Bible or the Web might help). List these in your book or a journal. Circle the names that have the greatest impact on you right now.

Bible Reference ɳoʈes

Use these notes to deepen your understanding as you study the Bible on your own:

Exodus 3:1-3

3:1 shepherding the flock. The call of God came to Moses to lead Israel. Like David he went from the role of shepherd to leader of God's flock (2 Sam. 7:8). **Jethro.** Another name for Reuel (2:18). The story of Moses' marriage is found in Exodus 2:16-22. **Horeb, the mountain of God.** Another name for Mount Sinai, to which the Israelites would return after being freed (v. 12; 19:1-2).

3:2 Angel of the LORD. Here the Angel of the Lord appeared, later it is the Lord (v. 4), and finally God (v. 4). It seems that each is describing God Himself.

Exodus 3:4-6

3:5 holy ground. The earth itself wasn't holy; God made it holy by being there. Everything and everyone that is near to God must be made holy—purified of imperfection.

3:6 afraid to look at God. To see God's face, Israelites believed, was to die (Gen. 16:13; 32:30). In 19:3, Moses met with God again on this very mountain. Moses discovered a relationship with God that made him unafraid (33:11), and at that point, Moses even called on God to "let me see Your glory" (33:18).

Exodus 3:7-10

3:8 I have come down to rescue. Picture God coming down out of heaven to work on behalf of His people. This "rescue" had been the source of the nation's prayers for many years (2:23). **land flowing with milk and honey.** This was a common way of describing the beautiful landscape of Canaan.

Exodus 3:11-12

3:11 Who am I. Moses several times expressed a desire not to be the one chosen to speak to Pharaoh (4:1,10,13). He may have wondered why God would send him back to the land where he had so many memories—including having committed murder, and where he had been a wanted man (2:15).

3:12 I will certainly be with you. Moses may have wondered "who" he was to be the deliverer (v. 11), but God's answer had nothing to do with Moses. Instead, God simply promised His presence with His servant. With God, Moses could accomplish anything God desired. **this will be the sign.** God offers proof that He would certainly accomplish His word. When the people came out of Egypt, they did indeed "worship God on this mountain" (v. 1; 19:1-2; Sinai is another name for Horeb).

Exodus 3:13-15

3:13 What is His name? Moses surely had learned about the Hebrew God, but he had been raised in Egypt—a land with many gods, all with different names. Moses asked God for His name.

3:14 I AM WHO I AM. This astonishing name God used for Himself expresses God's character as eternal, dependable, and faithful. **I AM.** In John 8:53-58, Jesus used this phrase to describe Himself, identifying Himself as God. In John 18:6, the power of the words "I am He," caused His captors to fall to the ground.

3:15 Yahweh. The Jewish scribes did not preserve the vowels for God's name, but Yahweh is almost certainly the correct pronunciation. Yahweh is related to the verb "I am" and is translated LORD.

Session

2

UNDONE:
HOW DO WE RESPOND TO GOD?

Connections Prep

MAIN LIFEPOINT:
God is not apathetic about our needs nor deaf to our requests. He allows us to have very real encounters with Him that should change our priorities and the way we live.

To reinforce the LifePoint, leaders and small-group facilitators should understand the following more detailed CheckPoints and "Do" Points.

BIBLE STUDY CHECKPOINTS:
· Examine Isaiah's experience with God and relate it to our own
· Understand Isaiah's response to God
· Evaluate how genuine encounters with God change lives

LIFE CHANGE "DO" POINTS:
· Commit to seeking God whole-heartedly
· Focus on consistent Bible study that reveals the true nature of God
· Learn to respond consistently to God's work in our lives

PREPARATION:
☐ Review the *Leader's Manual* for this session and prepare your teaching.
☐ Determine how you will subdivide students into small discussion groups.
☐ Recruit mature students or adults as small-group facilitators. Be sure these facilitators plan to attend.

REQUIRED SUPPLIES:
☐ *Essential Truth: Inviting Christ into My Reality* Leader books for each group facilitator
☐ *Essential Truth: Inviting Christ into My Reality* Student books for each student
☐ Pens or pencils for each student
☐ A pair of scissors for each small group

Get Ready

Read one these short Bible passages each day, and spend a few minutes of focused time with God. Be sure to jot down any insights you receive.

MONDAY

Read Isaiah 6:1-5
The vision described in these verses is hardly common. Do you ever have visions or dreams? What do you remember about them? Do they affect you the way this one impacted Isaiah?

TUESDAY

Read Revelation 1:9-20
Do you ever compare your experiences to those of others? How did John's experience on the island of Patmos compare with Isaiah's vision?

WEDNESDAY

Read Isaiah 6:6-7
Do you ever feel guilty? In your journal or in your prayers, confess some of the things you feel guilty about. How do you think God responds to our guilt and confessions?

THURSDAY

Read Revelation 5:1-5
The Bible explains that only Jesus can conquer sin. What emotions do you feel when you read this passage?

FRIDAY

Read Isaiah 6:8-10

When Isaiah encountered God, he responded, "Send me!" If God were to speak directly to you, how would you respond?

SATURDAY

Read Acts 8:26-29

Followers of Jesus often talk about how God speaks to them. Does God speak to you? Through what or whom does He speak? What do you do with the messages you receive?

2

SUNDAY

Read Acts 8:30-35

Phillip encountered an Ethiopian man who desperately wanted to understand God's Word. When you read the Bible, do you have a hard time understanding what you're reading? Do you ask for help or give up? How important is it to correctly interpret the Bible in order to respond to God's guidance for your life?

LARGE-GROUP OPENING:
Get everyone's attention. Make announcements. Open your session with a prayer. Read the LifePoint to the students.

 LifePoint

God is not apathetic about our needs nor deaf to our requests. He allows us to have very real encounters with Him that should change our priorities and the way we live.

SMALL-GROUP TIME:
Instruct students to separate into smaller groups of 4-8, preferably in a circle configuration. Call on the mature student or adult leaders you recruited to facilitate each small group through this "Say What?" segment.

Say What? *(15 MINUTES)*

Random Question of the Week:

If the Number 2 pencil is the most popular, then why is it Number 2?

Group Experience: Crossed or Uncrossed?

Try this deceptively simple "brain teaser" using:
- · A pair of scissors
- · Your dramatic flair

Arrange your group in a large circle. Hold up a pair of scissors and explain that everyone is going to have to figure out by your motions whether or not the scissors are "crossed" or "uncrossed." Immediately begin making elaborate motions with the scissors: point them in different directions and open and close them several times each time declaring "crossed" or "uncrossed." Here's the catch ... what you say has nothing to do with the scissors themselves. It has to do with whether or not your legs are crossed or uncrossed. Try to be sly about this at first, but if the students have a hard time catching on, be a bit more obvious.

As some of the students seem to catch on, pass the scissors to your left. Instruct the student to do as you've done, declaring the scissors "crossed" or "uncrossed." Give the students the "thumbs up" (if their legs are crossed) or the "thumbs down" (if their legs are not). If they figure the game out, be sure to tell them to hold their secret with you until the end. You should be able to go around the group a couple of times and watch as some students catch on and others get frustrated! After you are done, reveal that "crossed" or "uncrossed" had nothing to do with the scissors, but with the position of your legs!

After the exercise, ask these follow-up questions:

1. How did this game make you feel?

2. Crossed or Uncrossed" can be a pretty frustrating game until you get it. Then the whole thing seems so easy that you can't believe it took you so long to get it. How is life like that?

3. Is it difficult for you to get a picture of who God really is? Would it help if you saw a vision of God or audibly heard His voice? How do you think you'd respond if you "got it" and saw God for who He really is?

So What? *(30 MINUTES)*

Teaching Outline

2

I. Life-changing encounters
    A. We are enamored with celebrities
    B. Encounters with celebrities do not change our lives
    C. God, the greatest celebrity of all is interested in you & wants you to have personal encounters with Him
    D. We hear what we listen for (cricket story)

II. Key events shape our lives
    A. Isaiah – the year King Uzziah died
    B. Today – Terrorist attacks (9-11), tsunamis, hurricanes
    C. God often uses moments of confusion and questioning to grab our attention

III. God speaks to us – 4 avenues through which we "hear" God
    A. The Bible (God-breathed)
    B. Focused times of prayer (questions to God, dialog with our hearts, listen to the Holy Spirit)
    C. Other people (seek counsel and be open to "friends of God")
    D. Circumstances, nature, art, movies, etc.

IV. An encounter with God may lead to feelings of being overwhelmed, sinful, and "undone"
    A. Like Isaiah, we cannot stand in the presence of God (awesome & perfect)
    B. You cannot walk away the same

V. When God speaks we are changed!
    A. Because we have failed Him we deserve death, but He gives life
    B. The "hot coal" is a symbol of purifying power
    C. Through Jesus we are forgiven, healed, & changed forever
    D. Then we are given a mission & a purpose

**TEACHING FOR THE
LARGE GROUP**

A Celebrity Encounter

What would you do if your favorite celebrity walked up to you, introduced himself, and told you that he cared about your life story and had great plans for you? Our society worships celebrities. If you don't believe it, just take a look at the tabloids surrounding the checkout line at your favorite store. Entire industries are built around offering the general public a peek at the lives of the rich and famous. A person who spots a celebrity, whether it is a sports figure, a singer, or an actor will talk about it for weeks. We believe that fame is somehow equated with importance. But ❶ celebrity encounters—while they make for great stories—rarely change lives. What if someone far more famous than all of Hollywood's elite combined wanted you to encounter Him in a way that would change your life forever? How would it feel to learn that God who created everything had a personal interest in and plan for you? That's the kind of experience Isaiah had in Isaiah 6. And today we'll discuss that encounter as we look for answers the question: "How should we ❷ respond to God when He reveals Himself to us?"

❶ Celebrity encounters rarely *change lives*.

❷ Today we'll look for answers the question: How should we *respond* to God when He reveals Himself to us?

We Hear What We Listen For

An important attitude for us in listening to God is our readiness to hear Him. A story is told of two men who are walking along a crowded city sidewalk. Suddenly one of them said, "Listen to the musical sound of that cricket." His friend could not hear the sound. He asked, "How can you make out the sound of cricket in the roar of traffic and people everywhere?" The first man, a zoologist, had trained himself to hear the sound of nature, but did not explain. He simply dropped a coin from his pocket onto the sidewalk and pointed out a dozen people who turned to look. Then he explained, "We hear what we listen for." So, what are you listening for?

Learning from the Bible

Learning from the Bible ...

Isaiah 6:1-10

Ask for three volunteers to come to the front and read the parts of (1) Isaiah, (2) the seraphim, and (3) the Lord.

[ISAIAH] *¹ In the year that King Uzziah died, I saw the Lord seated on a high and lofty throne, and His robe filled the temple. ² Seraphim were standing above Him; each one had six wings: with two he covered his face, with two he covered his feet, and with two he flew. ³ And one called to another:*
[SERAPHIM] *Holy, holy, holy is the Lord of Hosts; His glory fills the whole earth.*
⁴ The foundations of the doorways shook at the sound of their voices, and the temple was filled with smoke.
[ISAIAH] *⁵ Then I said: Woe is me, for I am ruined, because I am a man of unclean lips and live among a people of unclean lips, [and] because my eyes have seen the King, the Lord of Hosts. ⁶ Then one of the seraphim flew to me, and in his hand was a glowing coal that he had taken from the altar with tongs. ⁷ He touched my mouth [with it] and said:*

[SERAPHIM] Now that this has touched your lips, your wickedness is removed, and your sin is atoned for.
[ISAIAH] ⁸ Then I heard the voice of the Lord saying:
[LORD] Who should I send? Who will go for Us?
[ISAIAH] I said: Here I am. Send me. ⁹ And He replied:
[LORD] Go! Say to these people: Keep listening, but do not understand; keep looking, but do not perceive. ¹⁰ Dull these people's minds of the people; deafen their ears and blind their eyes; otherwise they might see with their eyes and hear with their ears, understand with their mind, turn back, and be healed.

LARGE-GROUP TIME CONTINUED:
This is the meat of the teaching time. Remind students to follow along and take notes in their *Student Books*.

As you share the "So What?" information with students, make it your own. Use your natural teaching style.

Emphasize underlined information, which gives key points, answers to the *Student Book* questions or fill-in-the-blanks in the (shown in your margins).

Isaiah's recollection of his encounter with God helps to explain how we should respond when God speaks to our hearts. It also helps us to understand how God communicates.

A Starting Place

In the days of the ancient Hebrews, people dated things around certain pivotal events in history. Isaiah says, "In the year that King Uzziah died ..." For the people of Israel, the passing of a king was a major event. Not only would they mourn the loss of their leader, but the event itself would usher in a period of uncertainty as well. Political alliances were very loose and unstable in the ancient world, so the people—perhaps Isaiah included—had lots of fears, doubts, and questions about the future. Key events shape our lives as well. With our form of government, we can't relate to the impact of a king's death, but we can point to certain pivotal events that change the world in an instant. Where were you when the terrorist attacks of September 11 happened or a deadly tsunami or hurricane? How did you first hear about them? What were you doing? What was your immediate reaction? Have there been other key milestones or memories in your life that have left an impact on you? Often God uses moments of confusion and questioning to grab our attention. Our questions and uncertainty put us emotionally at a place where we are more willing to hear from God than we were just a few days or even a few moments ago.

There is no doubt that God got Isaiah's attention with the experience he relates in this passage. But what can we learn from it?

(1) God speaks to His followers.

When we encounter a passage of the Bible like this, one of our first reactions is to note that God may have given Isaiah this vision, but He has never spoken to you or me like that. So, just how does God speak to us? First, remember that even in biblical times it was rare for someone to hear an audible voice from God or have the type of experience that Isaiah did. With a handful of exceptions (Jesus, Abraham,

Moses, the Apostle John, and others), God usually connects with His people in a variety of ways. If there was anyone who deserved to hear an explanation for what he was going through, it was Job. Yet, even he noted many centuries ago, "For God speaks time and again, but a person may not notice it." (Job 33:14)

So, have you ever encountered God? How does God usually speak to us? ❸ First, God uses the Bible to speak to us. The Book of Hebrews points out that "In the past God spoke to our forefathers through the prophets at many times and in various ways" (1:1 NIV). Throughout the period of biblical history, God, through the Holy Spirit, inspired many men to write down His truth and His story and literally reveals "God-breathed" truth to us (2 Timothy 3:16 NIV).

GOD IS PRESENT
❸ Through what four avenues might we "hear" God?
1. *The Bible*
2. *Focused times of prayer*
3. *Other people*
4. *Circumstances, nature, art, movies, etc.*

❸ Second, God speaks to us through focused times of prayer. We must regularly take our questions to God, open a dialog with our hearts to understand what we really believe in our innermost being, and allow the Holy Spirit to direct us and transform us.

❸ Third, God uses other people to speak to us. When God wanted a message delivered to his people in the Bible, He chose a human representative to do it. Isaiah was one such "prophet" or "mouthpiece" for God. Often the people God enlists to speak for Him are people called to that task full-time such as parents, pastors, student ministers, missionaries, and authors. But God also calls on everyday, ordinary people like you and I to touch the lives of others; these might include your small-group leader or your friends. You need to seek out wise counsel and be sensitive to those around you, especially those that you would consider "friends of God."

❸ Fourth, God uses circumstances, group interaction, nature, art, movies, and other ways to help shape us and speak to us. Sometimes circumstances are unique to us, and sometimes they are things that are happening in the world at that time. Paul heard God both through the "thorn in his flesh" (a physical ailment that kept him humble) and through having world events block his planned missionary travels and lead him somewhere else through the Holy Spirit. Likewise, God uses experience to lead us to hear His voice and recognize what He is doing in the world. Caution: Experience must always be grounded in the Bible as our ultimate truth-source.

(2) An Encounter with God May Lead to Feelings of Being Overwhelmed, Sinful, and "Undone."

We often think how incredible it would be to be present if God truly "showed up" (although we know He's already present) in all of His glory and power. We hear preachers get fired up about revival, and we pray that we will encounter God. But, have you ever thought about what would happen if God literally showed up

4 When God reveals His glory, people are often *overwhelmed*.

on a Sunday morning or a Wednesday night? We think that we would be excited, **4** but the consistent testimony of Scripture is that when God reveals His glory, people are overwhelmed. Moses hid his face. Elijah hid in a cave. Habakkuk trembled in fear at the vision God revealed of what He was about to do. The shepherds who saw the angels became so scared they were "like dead men." Isaiah was "ruined," "undone," "gone for," depending on what translation you read. Why? God is perfect and holy, and we are not. While we may think we match up pretty well when compared with other people, we are no match for God's perfection and holiness. In addition, an unholy creature cannot survive in the presence of a holy God. Truly seeing God in His majesty and splendor was simply too much for Isaiah, and it would be too much for us. Think about it. Which areas of your life would you be ashamed of if God showed up today? You cannot walk away the same!

(3) When God Speaks ... We are Changed!

5 What does the "hot coal" mentioned in the Isaiah passage symbolize?

6 Describe the pattern God uses to reach into the lives He will use for His purposes.

Once we are truly humbled before God as we confess our failures and admit we have no right to be in His presence, God finally has us where He wants us. We deserve death ... and yet He gives life. So, we are cured from ever thinking, "It's about us" because without Him, we would be lost, ruined, and hopeless. Here He takes care of Isaiah's failures and guilt with the touch of **5** a hot coal, which symbolizes the purifying power of God to forgive and refine our impure lives. Of course, this is an echo of the great forgiveness and healing to come through Jesus, but the results are the same – life change. Isaiah is never again the same. He is "commissioned" and ready to go wherever God leads. **6** There is a certain pattern and process that God uses to reach into the lives He will use for His purposes: (1) we encounter God, (2) we're humbled, (3) we're forgiven and restored, and then (4) we're given a mission and a purpose. It's important to note that God didn't ask Isaiah to go somewhere specific. He asked, "Who will go for Us?" (Note the Hebrew plural, which is a reference to the Trinity) Are we genuinely changed and humbled by our encounters with God? Will we trust Him to send us even if He doesn't tell us up front exactly where He is leading?

SMALL-GROUP TIME:
Use this time to help students begin to integrate the truth they've learned into their lives while they connect with the other students in the group, the leaders, and with God.

After presenting the teaching material, ask students to divide back into small groups and discuss the "Do What?" questions. Small group facilitators should lead the discussions and set the tone by being open and honest in responding to each question.

Do What? *(15 MINUTES)*

Making It Personal

1. Isaiah described the people around him as "people of unclean lips." How would you describe the friends you spend the majority of your time with?

   ☐ Good all-around kids   ☐ Supportive – there for me no matter what
   ☐ Good Listeners   ☐ Backstabbers
   ☐ Manipulators   ☐ They defy categorizing – they are all types!
   ☐ Other: _____

2. What about God? How would you describe Him?

3. Which of the following do you have the most trouble understanding about God? Explain your struggle.

   ☐ Why God allows so much suffering
   ☐ What God wants me to do with my life
   ☐ Why God made me the way He did
   ☐ Why God doesn't speak and act in more obvious ways
   ☐ What God is planning for the future

4. Do you believe God wants to help you understand? If not, why? If so, how might He choose to speak to you?

5. Complete this sentence with the ending that is most true for you and tell why: "For me to believe that God was really speaking to me, as He did to Isaiah ...

   ☐ I would have to hear an audible voice.
   ☐ His words would have to be accompanied by a miracle.
   ☐ I would have to have a way to verify everything said.
   ☐ I would need to feel it to be true inside of me.
   ☐ His words would have to be consistent with the Bible.
   ☐ Other: _____

Small-group facilitators
should reinforce the
LifePoint for this ses-
sion. Make sure that
student's questions are
invited and addressed
honestly.

 # LifePoint Review

God is not apathetic about our needs nor deaf to our requests.He allows us to have very real encounters with Him that should change our priorities and the way we live.

"Do" Points:

These "Do" Points will help you begin to experience this week's LifePoint. Be open and honest as you answer the questions within your small group.

1. <u>Commit to seek God with all your heart.</u> You will know you have met the living God in the way that Isaiah did if you are blown away by your encounter with Him and your life is changed forever. **Are you seeking God, the true God, with every fabric of who you are, or are you playing religious games with Him?**

2. <u>Focus on consistent Bible study that reveals the true nature of God.</u> The Bible is God's primary means of "revelation" of truth to us. As one Bible scholar states, "We don't read the Bible; it reads us. It doesn't tell us what we want to hear, but what we need to hear." We need God's guidance for our daily lives. **What attitudes do you need to grapple with that prevent you from making Bible study a consistent habit in your life?**

3. <u>Learn to respond consistently to God's work in your life.</u> God wants us to give Him our hopes, our dreams, and our plans. Amazingly, as we give our lives to God and trust Him we find that we're filled with more peace, joy, and excitement than we could ever have imagined. **What will it take for you to respond to God by accepting and trusting His plan for you instead of your own?**

Prayer Connection:

Be sure to end your
session by asking
students to share prayer
needs with one another,
especially as they relate
to issues brought up by
today's session.

This is the time to encourage, support, and pray for each other in our journeys to trust God and seek out real and personal encounters with Him.

Share prayer needs with the group, especially those related to hearing from and responding to God. Your group facilitator will close your time in prayer.

Encourage students to list prayer needs for others in their books so they can pray for one another during the week. Assign a student coordinator in each small group to gather the group's requests and e-mail them to the group members.

Prayer Needs:

Encourage students to dig a little deeper by completing a "Now What?" assignment before the next time you meet. Remind students about the "Get Ready" short daily Bible readings and related questions at the beginning of Session 3.

Remind them again this week that they are loved!

 # now What?

Deepen your understanding of who God is, and continue the journey you've begun today by choosing one of the following assignments to complete this week:

Option #1:
If you're artistic, use your talent to create a work of art based on Isaiah's vision of the throne room of God. For centuries, artists have been inspired by this otherworldly vision and imagined the majesty and "holy terror" of it in a number of creative and inspiring ways. Plan to share your painting, photographs, sketch, or sculpture with your small group next week.

Option #2:
For centuries, those who have led church services have used Isaiah 6 as a model for planning a time of corporate worship. With some help from your friends or small group, plan a student worship service around the following elements from Isaiah 6. Choose songs, Scriptures, dramas, and personal stories that go with each.
- · Isaiah 6:1-4: God's Holiness
- · Isaiah 6:5: Our Brokenness
- · Isaiah 6:6-7: Forgiveness
- · Isaiah 6:8-9: Mission

Bible Reference Notes

Use these notes to deepen your understanding as you study the Bible on your own:

Isaiah 6:1-10

6:1 King Uzziah died. Uzziah, a good king who ruled well, reigned from 792 until he died in 740 B.C. He contracted leprosy as a judgment upon his insistence on burning incense in God's temple and died with that condition (2 Chron. 26:16-21). He was also known as Azariah (2 Chron. 26:1). The story of Isaiah's call validated his claim to be a spokesman for God.

6:2 Seraphim. These angels are mentioned by name only here in the Bible. Their name comes from a Hebrew word meaning "burn," possibly speaking of God's purity (v. 6; Rev. 4:6-9). Note the contrast between their worship of God and the rebellious pride of humanity.

6:3 Holy, holy, holy. Repeating a word three times in Hebrew means it is supremely important. God's holiness is indescribably perfect and transcendent. God is completely above us and different from us, and yet, in His mercy, He reaches us and cares for us.

6:5 my eyes have seen the King. Isaiah expresses concern because whoever sees God is expected to die, since humans are incapable of surviving the sight of God's majesty and glory (Gen. 32:30; Ex. 33:20). In the light of God's perfect holiness, Isaiah's sinful humanness stands in stark contrast.

6:6 glowing coal. The coals were kept burning on the altar outside of the temple with the fire God started in Leviticus 9:24. Isaiah's sin needed to be burned away by God's fire. This altar was where sacrifices were made to cleanse the people's sins.

6:7 He touched my mouth. God touches Isaiah's mouth to purify it in order to communicate His Word. (See also Jer. 1:9.)

6:8 Who will go for Us? The plural could refer to God speaking on behalf of Himself and His angelic host (Gen. 1:26; 3:22; 11:7), referring to Himself in the plural of majesty, or alluding to the Trinity: Father, Son, and Holy Spirit. In this case, Isaiah the prophet is made part of the divine decision. This prophetic honor was also given to Micaiah (1 Kings 22:19-20) and Jeremiah (23:18,22; Amos 3:7). **Here I am.** Like Abraham, Moses, and Samuel, Isaiah answers as a servant when God calls him by name. (See also Gen. 22:1; Ex. 3:4; 1 Sam. 3:4,6,8.) They all were willing to be available; to be whatever God wanted them to be.

6:9-10 Jesus made use of this passage in the parable of the sower (see Matt. 13:14-15; Mark 4:12; Luke 8:10; Rom. 11:7-10,25). **Dull the minds.** God knew that most of the people would not listen to Isaiah. His warnings did save some, but also served to increase the guilt of Judah, since the people rejected his message. According to Jewish tradition, Isaiah was sawn in two.

Acts 8:26-35

8:27 eunuch. Eunuchs (men who were castrated so they be trusted with royal women) were commonly employed as royal officials. Although attracted to Judaism, a eunuch would never be allowed to fully participate in the temple worship (Deut. 23:1). **Candace.** A dynastic title for the Ethiopian queens.

8:32-33 He was led like a sheep. The eunuch was reading from Isaiah 53:7-8, a key Old Testament passage describing Jesus as the "Suffering Servant" or "Servant of the Lord." This particular passage underlines much of what Luke has already recorded about the apostles' preaching concerning the identity of Jesus (3:13; 4:27).

8:34 who is the prophet saying this about? The eunuch's question was a common one in Jewish circles. Some thought the prophet was speaking of his own sufferings as one rejected, while others thought he was speaking figuratively of Israel as a nation that suffered at the hands of its oppressors (Isa. 44:1-2). Still another view of the Servant's identity linked him with Cyrus the King of Persia (see Isa. 44:28—45:1-3.) The traditional rabbis had not made any connection between the Suffering Servant of Isaiah 53, the kingly Messiah of Isaiah 11, and the glorified Son of Man in Daniel 13. Only in Jesus' teachings did these concepts finally come together (Luke 24:26).

8:35 the good news about Jesus. Philip used this passage as a jumping off point to explain the ministry of Jesus. He undoubtedly referred the eunuch to other verses in Isaiah 53 as well as the other references to the Servant in Isaiah that point out the Servant's suffering for the sake of others and how this Servant would be a light for the Gentiles. All of this would have been related to Jesus' ministry, death, and resurrection.

NOTES

Session

3

LOVE GOD, LOVE PEOPLE: WHAT DOES GOD EXPECT OF US?

Connections Prep

MAIN LIFEPOINT: Jesus clarified life's two greatest priorities for each of us: love God and love others.

To reinforce the LifePoint, leaders and small-group facilitators should understand the following more detailed CheckPoints and "Do" Points.

BIBLE STUDY CHECKPOINTS:
- Understand core biblical foundations that explain what matters to God
- Wrestle with priorities in view of God's expectations
- Grasp how God helps us to love Him and others

LIFE CHANGE "DO" POINTS:
- Develop a lifestyle of worship that involves a thankful heart
- Give God first priority of time, talents, and resources
- Express love for others through encouragement and service

PREPARATION:
- ☐ Review the *Leader's Book* for this session and prepare your teaching.
- ☐ <u>Option 1</u>: Connect with your Minister of Education or Sunday School Director to find out if your class could adopt a Sunday School class or group made up primarily of senior adults for this session.
- ☐ <u>Option 1</u>: Bring breakfast or snack foods (don't forget the doughnuts! and coffee!) to share with the senior adults and students in this session. Be sure to remember napkins, cups, and other supplies.
- ☐ Determine how you will subdivide students into small discussion groups.
- ☐ Recruit mature students or adults as small-group facilitators. Be sure these facilitators plan to attend.

REQUIRED SUPPLIES:
- ☐ *Essential Truth: Inviting Christ into My Reality* Leader books for each group facilitator
- ☐ *Essential Truth: Inviting Christ into My Reality* Student books for each student
- ☐ Pens or pencils for each student

Get Ready

Read one these short Bible passages each day, and spend a few minutes grabbing hold of what God really expects. Be sure to write down any insights God reveals to you.

MONDAY

Read 1 Corinthians 13:13

The term "love" has multiple applications in the English language. For instance, you may say you "love" hamburgers, or you might announce, "I love so-and-so." What kind of "love" does Paul describe in this passage, and why is it so important?

TUESDAY

Read 1 John 3:13-15

Hate language is blatantly offensive. Why does John use love-hate language to describe our relationship with the world? Can you think of an example of how love has counteracted death in your life or in that of a friend?

WEDNESDAY

Read 1 John 3:16-20

John prompts us to love in actions and in truth. Be specific: How can you demonstrate love in action and truth to someone in your world?

THURSDAY

Read 1 John 4:7-12

John describes God's nature as love. Our ability to love others comes from God. Think about the motivation behind your last act of kindness. Was it out of genuine love, or were you "loving" in order to get something you wanted? How can you keep your motives pure when demonstrating love?

FRIDAY

Read Exodus 20:1-17

Society is torn over whether or not to preserve the Ten Commandments on court-house and schoolroom walls, but few people who argue against their posting know what they say. Can you recite the Ten Commandments? Which of the ten is the most challenging for you to keep on a daily basis?

SATURDAY

Read Mark 12:28-31

Jesus often replied to those questioning Him with words from the Scripture. What stands out to you about the two commandments He chose as His answer here?

3

SUNDAY

Read Mark 12:32-34

Jesus reversed His role with the teacher of the law in just a few sentences. What can we expect from God when we seek answers to questions we have about Him and what He says in the Bible?

LARGE-GROUP OPENING:
Get everyone's attention. Make announcements. Open your session with a prayer. Read the LifePoint to the students.

 LifePoint

Jesus clarified life's two greatest priorities for each of us: love God and love others.

SMALL-GROUP TIME:
Instruct students to
separate into smaller
groups of 4-8, prefer-
ably in a circle con-
figuration. Call on the
mature student or adult
leaders you recruited
to facilitate each small
group through this "Say
What?" segment.

This week you have
two options for your
time together as a
group. Option one
will be much more
challenging and expe-
riential, but it has
the potential for the
greatest impact. The
second option is more
simplistic, but it can
work with less
preparation and time.

Say What? *(15 MINUTES)*

Random Question of the Week:

Apples aren't called "reds." Bananas aren't called "yellows." So why are oranges called "oranges"?

Group Experience: Loving Your Neighbors

Option #1: Adopt-a-Senior Group or Class

Sociologists have noted that when it comes to values, this generation of students has more in common with their grandparents than their parents. This means that, despite initial fears, students connect well with senior adults. In addition, senior citizens that are in every church and community often feel forgotten, neglected, and disconnected from young people. With the help of their group leader or teacher, plan to integrate the senior adults into your study for the day. Here are some suggestions to make the opportunity meaningful:

- Provide some breakfast or snack foods (don't forget the doughnuts! and coffee!) to share with the senior adults. Be sure to remember napkins, cups, etc.
- Carefully integrate the "small group times" to ensure that senior adults are mixed with students.
- For an icebreaker, have everyone get something to eat and then sit in small groups. Ask each senior adult to briefly share what he or she loved most about being a teenager. Have each student briefly share what he or she is most looking forward to about the future.
- If possible, choose several students to help you teach the lesson that follows. Senior adults love to hear from young people, and especially those who are growing in Christ. It reminds them that their legacy is secure and all their efforts within the church have not been in vain — there is another generation emerging that loves God!
- Close the end of you session today by asking the senior adults to pray for the students. Then ask the students to pray for the senior adults.

After the session is over, be sure to find some time to debrief with your students. Ask them what it was like to combine their love for God with loving people! Listen to their stories and challenge them to find more ways to love the "neighbors" who are around them everyday!

After the experience, discuss the following questions:

1. What was it like to combine love for God with loving people?

2. Would you like to share a story from our "Say What?" experience?

Option #2: Adopt-a-Neighbor

1. Who are the literal neighbors that live around where your group meets? As a group, brainstorm a list of neighbors.

2. Then choose one and make plans to serve that neighbor. Examples of neighbors and loving actions you might suggest to your students include:

   · If your church is located in a downtown area and you meet at a church, there might be residents who live nearby who need yard work done. If there are businesses nearby, offer to wash windows or mop floors.
   · If your meeting room is in a church and there are other classes around, treat a neighboring class with kindness. Offer to clean their room and have students bring food and treats to share with that class. If it's a preschool room, offer to help pick up toys, take children to the playground to give the teachers a breather, etc. Be sure to let them know you are coming so you don't disturb an important moment!
   · If you meet off campus in a host home or coffee shop, try to find a way to serve someone in your neighborhood that will be a meaningful act for your group.

3. How do you think people would respond to random acts of love and kindness like the ones you're discussing?

LARGE-GROUP TIME:
Have the students turn
to face the front for this
teaching time. Be sure
you can make eye con-
tact with each student
in the room. Encourage
students to follow
along and take notes in
their *Student Books*.

 # So What? *(30 MINUTES)*

Teaching Outline

I. What Does God Expect of Us?

A. A major point of differing opinion among world religions

B. Gods & goddesses in most ancient religions had no expectations of people
(e.g. Greek gods and goddesses immoral & paid little attention to humanity)

C. In today's religions "gods" often make ridiculously strict demands

1. Islam – perfectly obey "Allah;" 5 Pillars of Islam; pilgrimages; jihad

2. Buddhism - meditate constantly & live peaceful lives

3. Hinduism - good karma; ancestor worship; bathe in filthy River Ganges

4. New Age - get in touch with inner self; meditate; powers of crystals

5. Judaism - rigid adherence to a set of laws to make God happy

D. Christianity: *only* faith about God getting closer to man; He doesn't expect
rigid adherence to a set of rules, but obedient love and loyalty

II. What It Means to Be a Christ-Follower

A. What God cares most about is *people*—not institutions or rules

B. KEY #1: Loving God is the foundation of our faith

1. The "Shema" (Deut. 6:4-7)

2. Mark 12:30 quoted (see Ex. 20:3) – summarizes Ten Commandments

3. First 4 commandments – "Loving God with all your heart"

4. Other 6 commandments – "Love your neighbor as yourself"

5. How well do you know Scripture? (deepens your relationship with Him)

C. KEY #2: Loving God is a way of life, not just a Sunday thing

1. God has made the first move to know & love us

2. Jeremiah 1:5 – God handpicked you before you were born

3. Won't put anything or anyone above Him (Ex. 20:4-6)

4. Won't disrespect Him or His name (Ex. 20:7)

5. Set aside time to focus on Him on a regular basis (Ex. 20:8-11)

6. How does your life reflect your love for God?

D. KEY #3: We're able to love others out of the overflow of God's love to us

1. Our "neighbors" include everyone God has involved in our lives

2. When we respond to God's love, our hearts cannot hold this love inside

3. Ways to show love (commandments of Ex. 20:12-17)

4. How do your relationships with others reflect your love for God?

Share the "So What?"
teaching with your stu-
dents. You may modify
it to meet your needs.

Be sure to highlight
the underlined infor-
mation, which gives
answers to the *Student
Book* questions and fill-
in-the-blanks (shown in
your margins).

TEACHING FOR THE LARGE GROUP

❶ What question summarizes one major point of differing opinion among world religions?

❷ Islam teaches that people are to *pray* to Mecca several times daily, follow the *Five Pillars of Islam*, go on a *pilgrimage* to Mecca, and even, in radical instances, carry out *jihad* (holy war).

❸ Buddhism insists that worshipers *meditate* constantly and live peaceful lives.

❹ Hinduism stresses that people should work to build good *karma*, should worship ancestors *reincarnated* in the form of animals, and even *bathe* in the filthy River Ganges.

❺ New Age Movements insist that people should get in touch with their *inner selves*, *meditate*, and call upon the powers of *crystals*.

❻ Judaism stresses rigid adherence to a set of *laws*.

❼ God doesn't expect rigid adherence to a set of rules. He expects obedient *love* and *loyalty*.

What Does God Expect of Us?

❶ <u>One major point of differing opinion among world religions involves the question: "What does God expects of us?"</u> Before Judaism, most religions in the ancient world did not proclaim that gods and goddesses had many expectations of people. For instance, the Greek gods and goddesses were portrayed in lots of immoral behavior. They lied, committed adultery, and killed; they were so wrapped up in their own issues that they paid little attention to humanity. Even today's major religions differ from the Judeo-Christian view. In today's cases, however, the "gods" often make ridiculously strict demands on humanity.

3

❷ Islam teaches that god or "Allah" must be perfectly obeyed. People are to <u>pray</u> to Mecca several times daily, follow the <u>Five Pillars of Islam</u>, go on a <u>pilgrimage</u> to Mecca, and even, in radical instances, carry out <u>jihad</u> (holy war).

❸ Buddhism insists that worshipers <u>meditate</u> constantly and live peaceful lives.

❹ Hinduism stresses that people should work to build good <u>karma</u>, worship ancestors reincarnated in the form of animals, and even bathe in the filthy River Ganges.

❺ New Age Movements insist that people should get in touch with their <u>inner selves, meditate</u>, and call upon the powers of <u>crystals and other objects</u>.

❻ Even Judaism, the foundation of the Christian faith, stresses rigid adherence to a set of <u>laws</u>. Humans are to follow these laws to make God happy. They are to strictly observe the Sabbath, enforce harsh dietary restrictions, and offer sacrifices for their sins.

Christianity is the *only* world faith that is not about man getting closer to God, but about God getting closer to man. Because God loved you first, your heart's desire should be to willingly do anything for Him—not because He demands it of you, but because you love Him. ❼ <u>God doesn't expect a rigid adherence to a set of rules. He expects obedient love and loyalty</u>. Let's see how Jesus explained this.

Learning from the Bible

28 One of the scribes approached. When he heard them debating and saw that Jesus answered them well, he asked Him, "Which commandment is the most important of all?"
29 "This is the most important," Jesus answered:
Listen, Israel! The Lord our God, The Lord is One. 30 Love the Lord your God with all your heart, with all your soul, with all your mind, and with all your strength.

Learning from
the Bible ...
Mark 12:28-34

You may read the
passage yourself or ask
a volunteer to come to
the front of the room
and read it.

LARGE-GROUP TIME
CONTINUED:
This is the meat of the
teaching time. Remind
students to follow along
and take notes in their
Student Books.

As you share the
"So What?" information
with students, make
it your own. Use your
natural teaching style.

Emphasize underlined
information, which gives
key points, answers to
the *Student Book*
questions or fill-in-the-
blanks in the (shown in
your margins).

❽ What God cares most
about is *people*—not
institutions or rules.

³¹ *"The second is: Love your neighbor as yourself. There is no other commandment greater than these."*
³² *Then the scribe said to Him, "You are right, Teacher! You have correctly said that He is One, and there is no one else except Him.* ³³ *And to love Him with all your heart, with all your understanding, and to love your neighbor as yourself, is far more important than all the burnt offerings and sacrifices."*
³⁴ *When Jesus saw that he answered intelligently, He said to him, "You are not far from the kingdom of God." And no one dared to question Him any longer.*

What It Means to Be a Christ-Follower
The Christian faith has many core teachings that at first seem simple, but a closer look reveals that they are not. Jesus' responses to His critics reveal valuable insights into what it means to be a true Christ-follower.

What does God expect of us? Opinions on that debate have raged since the days of Cain and Abel. As most world religions develop, they become very complex in the code of laws and rules that must be obeyed in order to please the gods or god. This was the case in first-century Judea. Jesus recognized that the Jews had all of the outward trappings of religion, but they had forgotten about the relationship they were supposed to have with God. One of the benchmarks of Jesus' earthly ministry was His ability to cut through religious charades, getting to the heart of the matter. Consistently, He demonstrated that what ❽ God cares about most is people—not institutions or rules ... people. One of the most important connections made in the New Testament is the link between loving God and loving the people around us.

There are three keys to understanding what is expected of us as Christ-followers in Jesus' response to the teachers of the law.

God is a Mystery
(1) ❾ Loving God is the foundation of our faith.
Jesus begins His response with what is known to the Jews as the "Shema" (see Deuteronomy 6:4-7) and then quotes another Scripture that basically summarizes all Ten Commandments. The first four commandments all center on the idea of "Loving the Lord your God with all your heart" (Mark 12:30; Exodus 20:3). Misusing the name of God and failing to keep a day set aside for God are all commandments that violate the first: "Have no other gods before the Lord your God." Likewise, "Love your neighbor as yourself" summarizes the next six. Jesus interpreted Scripture as God intended it and responded to the Pharisees with the core truths of their own foundational teachings.

❾ List the three keys to understanding what is expected of us as Christ-followers that are revealed in Jesus' response to the teachers of the law.

1)_____

2)_____

3)_____

How well do you know Scripture? Can you handle it properly? How do you respond to those who try to trap or attack you in matters of faith? Having a firm grasp of God's teachings is critical to becoming the best Christ-follower you can be. Knowing what God's Word says will also help you deepen your love relationship with Him.

(2) ❾ Loving God is a way of life, not just something that happens on Sundays.

We don't make the first move towards God; He has made the first move to know and love us. Jeremiah 1:5 says that God handpicked you before you were even born. People who love God will not put anything or anyone else above Him (Exodus 20:4-6), nor will they disrespect Him or His name (Exodus 20:7). Loving God means setting aside time to focus on Him on a regular basis (Exodus 20:8-11). Because of a church culture that sometimes mirrors societal values too much, many Christians have settled into believing that "loving God" is something we do on Sundays instead of recognizing it as a way of life. God cannot be put in a box! If you limit your love of God to just a few hours a week, honoring Him only for an hour or two on Sunday morning, you are missing out on so much that He has for you!

Those who truly love God will show Him devotion throughout the week. They will declare and demonstrate their love for Him at home, at school, at work, and throughout life's busyness. What about you? How does your life reflect your love for God?

(3) ❾ We are able to love other people out of the overflow of God's love in our own lives.

Our "neighbors" include everyone God has involved in our lives. When we truly respond to the great love of God, our hearts and lives simply cannot hold the love inside. That love spills out of us into the lives of all those with whom we come in contact. As one pastor noted, "Just as you can't hold the great, furious waters of the raging ocean in a single thimble, so the great love of God cannot be contained within a single human heart."

People who truly love their neighbors show this love in a number of ways. They honor and respect their families ... especially their parents who provide for them. They don't bring harm to others. They don't violate or manipulate other people for personal pleasure. They don't desire or take what is not theirs to begin with. And they don't lie and live bitterly (the commandments of Exodus 20:12-17). How do your relationships with others reflect your love for God?

SMALL-GROUP TIME:
Use this time to help
students begin to inte-
grate the truth they've
learned into their lives
while they connect with
the other students in the
group, the leaders, and
with God.

After the teaching ses-
sion, ask students to
divide back into small
groups and discuss the
"Do What?" questions.
Small-group facilitators
should lead the discus-
sions, encouraging
openness and affirming
any and all serious
responses.

 # Do What? *(15 MINUTES)*

Love Connections

1. When do you feel most connected to God? Give examples of how you experience His love. Explain how you return that love.

2. Describe your personal commitment to reaching out to others in love. Why do you think people generally have a hard time getting outside the church box to reach out to others? How might we be able to overcome these struggles?

3. It's a challenge to make loving others a way of life. Which "neighbors" are hardest for you to love?
   - ☐ The people who live across the street from me
   - ☐ The kids I go to school with
   - ☐ My parents
   - ☐ My brothers and sisters
   - ☐ Those who have hurt me
   - ☐ Those who ignore me
   - ☐ Other: _____

Small-group facilitators
should reinforce the
LifePoint for this ses-
sion. Make sure that
student's questions are
invited and addressed
honestly.

 # LifePoint Review

Jesus clarified life's two greatest priorities for each of us: loveGod and love others.

"Do" Points:

These "Do" Points will help you grab hold of this week's LifePoint. Be with yourself and others as you answer the questions within your small group.

1. <u>Develop a lifestyle of worship that involves a thankful heart.</u> The Bible teaches (Romans 12:1-2) and demonstrates through the lives of God's people (Habakkuk 3:16-19) that worship is a way of life. **What might it look like to love God with all of your heart, soul, mind, and strength?**

2. <u>Give God first priority of your time, talent, and resources.</u> We give our time to what we love most. The ways we use our talents and resources shed light on what really matters to us. **Is God your first priority when it comes to your time? How can you use your talents and abilities in a way that God gets the very first priority in your life?**

3. <u>Express love for others through encouragement and service.</u> When Christ-followers give their lives away through service to others, they earn the right to be heard. **What can you do this week to show someone who doesn't believe in Jesus that you care? Why is it important that you do?**

Be sure to end your session by asking students to share prayer needs with one another, especially as they relate to issues brought up by today's session.

Encourage students to list prayer needs for others in their books so they can pray for one another during the week. Assign a student coordinator in each small group to gather the group's requests and e-mail them to the group members.

Prayer Connection:

This is the time to encourage, support, and pray for each other in our journeys to grasp God's love for us and to understand how important it is that we respond to His love and share it with others.

Share prayer needs with the group. Your group facilitator will close your time in prayer.

Prayer Needs:

 **now What?**

Encourage students to dig a little deeper by completing a "Now What?" assignment before the next time you meet. Remind students about the "Get Ready" short daily Bible readings and related questions at the beginning of Session 4.

Remind them that because they are so loved, they can share that love with others!

Option #1:

If you discussed a "neighbor" project in the "Say What? segment, set a time as a group to complete that project. Be sure to communicate to this neighbor that you expect nothing in return. Simply say (if they ask) that they are "friends of God." After the experience is over, be sure to find some time to debrief as a group. What was it like to combine your love for God with loving people?

Option #2:

Invest in a new friend—guys find a new guy to hang out with; girls, find a new gal pal. Find ways you can build a relationship with someone at school or work, or perhaps a senior adult in your church. Offer to take this person out for a soft drink or a burger. Use the outing to get to know his or her story.

Option #3:

Read a great book about loving God and others Here are a few suggestions:

- *Experiencing God* by Henry Blackaby will help you get your arms around the idea that God is up to something. You can join Him where He's at work.

- *Praise Habit* by David Crowder examines how expressing love to God should become a natural part of our everyday lives. Crowder, a modern worship leader, walks through Psalms to get insight into the mind and heart of David.

- *Conspiracy of Kindness* by Stephen Sjogren gives biblical foundation and suggestions for ways to reach into our communities and truly love our neighbors.

Bible Reference notes

Use these notes to deepen your understanding as you study the Bible on your own:

Mark 12:28-34

2:28 scribes. Jesus has answered successfully the Herodians, the Pharisees, and the Sadducees. It is now a scribe's turn to ask a question. His attitude toward Jesus is different from the others. He asks a genuine question. **saw that Jesus answered them well.** This teacher of the law is very impressed with the way Jesus answered the questions, so he asks an important question for Him personally. **Which commandment is the most important?** This phrase is, literally, "which is the chief (or first) commandment"; i.e., what commandment summarizes all the commandments?

12:29 Listen, Israel! The Shema (a statement of faith taken from Deut. 6:4), is recited by pious Jews each morning and evening. This affirmation captures what was clearly distinctive about Israel's God.

12:30 Love. In Greek, this is agape. It means an active, benevolent giving to others without expectation of reward. **heart.** The inner life; the center of personality; where God reveals Himself to a person. **soul.** The seat of life itself; the personality or ego. **mind.** The organ of knowledge; the intellect. **strength.** The power of a living being; the total effort behind heart, soul, and mind.

12:31 Jesus now quotes Leviticus 19:18, and in doing so connects loving God with loving people.

12:33 far more important than all the burnt offerings and sacrifices. This teacher was probably a student of the great prophets, whose teaching is echoed in this statement (see Isa. 1:10-17; Amos 5:21-25; and Mic. 6:6-8)

Session

4

SOME OLD BOOK: WHY DOES THE BIBLE MATTER?

Connections Prep

MAIN LIFEPOINT: The Bible is more than a just an ancient book; its message, written by men under the inspiration of God, is alive and relevant today.

To reinforce the LifePoint, leaders and small-group facilitators should understand the following more detailed CheckPoints and "Do" Points.

BIBLE STUDY CHECKPOINTS:
· Understand why the Bible is more than just a book
· Discover that the Bible can reveal God's best for us and teaches us how to deal with temptations
· Learn ways to guard against false interpretation of the Bible

LIFE CHANGE "DO" POINTS:
· Make personal Bible Study a consistent habit in our lives
· Commit to studying the Bible in community with other followers of Jesus
· Memorize Bible passages to get God's truth off the page and into our lives

PREPARATION:
☐ Review the *Leader's Book* for this session and prepare your teaching.
☐ Determine how you will subdivide students into small discussion groups.
☐ Recruit mature students or adults as small-group facilitators. Be sure these facilitators plan to attend.

REQUIRED SUPPLIES:
☐ *Essential Truth: Inviting Christ into My Reality* Leader books for each group facilitator
☐ *Essential Truth: Inviting Christ into My Reality* Student books for each student
☐ Pens or pencils for each student
☐ 3x5 cards or pieces of scratch paper for each student

Get Ready

Read one of these short Bible passages each day, and spend a few minutes wrapping your brain around it. Be sure to jot down any insights you discover as you spend time with God and His Word.

MONDAY

Read Deuteronomy 8:1-5

The Bible is an instructional guide for life. How can you be sure you don't forget its teachings? What should you do when you don't remember what God's Word says about a certain issue?

TUESDAY

Read Matthew 4:1-4

Jesus gave up food for 40 days. Why would a person do such a thing? What do you think motivated Jesus' actions?

WEDNESDAY

Read Psalm 91:9-13

The author of this psalm makes an "if-then" promise. What is it? What can we expect if we focus our hope on God and not ourselves?

THURSDAY

Read Matthew 4:5-7

Many people are surprised to discover that Satan knows what the Bible says. How might Satan twist the psalm you read yesterday to use it against Jesus?

FRIDAY   **Read Exodus 17:1-7**

God provided for His people, yet they wanted more. Do you always want more than what you've received? How can you keep yourself in check?

SATURDAY   **Read Matthew 4:8-11**

"Bow to me," Satan bribed Jesus, "and I will give you power." Are you ever tempted to "bow" to something or someone other than God? Why is it difficult to make pleasing God your first priority?

SUNDAY   **Read Deuteronomy 6:13-19**

Is this passage, "fear" refers to sacred respect rather than the emotion we typically associate with the word. What ways to "fear God" are outlined in these verses?

LARGE-GROUP OPENING:
Get everyone's attention. Make announcements. Open your session with a prayer. Read the LifePoint to the students.

 LifePoiNt

The Bible is more than a just an ancient book; its message, written by men under the inspiration of God, is alive and relevant today.

SMALL-GROUP TIME:
Instruct students to
separate into smaller
groups of 4-8, prefer-
ably in a circle con-
figuration. Call on the
mature student or adult
leaders you recruited
to facilitate each small
group through this "Say
What?" segment.

Say What? *(15 MINUTES)*

Random Question of the Week:
If a clown's purpose is to make people smile, why do some circus clowns paint frowns on their faces?

Group Experience: Two Truths and a Lie

Begin your small-group time with the following activity:

- Pens
- 3x5 cards or pieces of scratch paper for each person in the group
- Your best poker face

Give each student a 3x5 card or a small sheet of paper and pen. Instruct them to come up with three statements about themselves. The catch is that only two of them can be true. One should be completely made up. If your small group members know each other well, challenge them to come up with details of their lives that are likely unknown to the others. The statements can be simple (I have lived in Florida; Pizza is my favorite food). But the more creative the statements are, the better (I once met Michael Jordan in an airport; I have whitewater rafted the Snake River). Just make sure the statements are believable ("I once bungee jumped with the elastic out of my underwear" is entertaining, but not very convincing).

After allowing the students a few moments to write, go around the group and ask each person share his or her 3 statements. After each reading, have the group try to guess which of the statements was the lie. Acknowledge the student who is the best at identifying lies. Congratulate his or her ability to discern the truth.

After everyone has had a turn, ask the following:

1. Who told the most outrageous lie?

2. What was the most outrageous truth you heard?

3. Who was the most believable liar? Why was he or she so convincing?

4. What gave most people away? Did it have anything to do with how well you knew them?

Explain that today's lesson won't be able to answer all their questions, but stress how important it is for each of them to grapple with their issues until they know that the Bible can be trusted and used in their everyday lives.

After the questions are answered, hold up your Bible. Say something like, "In my hands I hold a book that has been more used, more abused, more studied, and more scrutinized than any other literary work in history. Some call it a lie. Others think it tells half-truths. But this book changes lives more than any other. This work that was compiled over literally thousands of years is more than a mere book, and Christians believe that every word in it is true. Today we're going to explore the Bible. We'll look at how Jesus used it, and we'll discover why it still matters today."

5. (As time permits ...) What issues or questions do you have concerning the Bible's authenticity.

LARGE-GROUP TIME: Have the students turn to face the front for this teaching time. Be sure you can make eye contact with each student in the room. Encourage students to follow along and take notes in their *Student Books*.

 # So What? *(30 MINUTES)*

Teaching Outline

I. An age of information overload
   A. Library of Congress has over 530 miles of bookshelves
   B. Find everything on the Net
   C. Bible by far the best-selling book ... does it still matter in 21st century?

II. The Breath of God
   A. The Bible is inspired ... the breath of life from God to us
   B. "Inspiration" carries the very authority of God
   C. "Revelation" is truth that God reveals to us for life
   D. The Bible is "infallible"—internally consistent & without error
   E. Provides instruction, encouragement, & direction for living

III. Jesus focused on following God's direction for His life & lived out the truth of Scripture
   A. To stay focused on God & His mission Jesus got away from crowds & distractions
   B. He also fasted from food
   C. We need to carve out time to hear from God

IV. Jesus prepared Himself for this desert challenge before it arrived

    A. He understood the importance of the Bible, memorizing & meditating on its truth

    B. He lived of lifetime of drawing closer to God & studying His Word

    C. We need to prepare of the unexpected challenges ahead

    D. God's words have spiritual power

V. Jesus' enemies know the Bible & distort it for their own ends

    A. The Devil knows the Bible & distorts it to deceive us and use it against us

    B. We defeat him by reciting the truth of the Bible and clinging to it

VI. 3 things to be sure that we're using God's Word correctly

    1) Develop a working knowledge of what the Bible says

    2) Discover whether the Scripture is being used consistently with the meaning it had in its original & total context

    3) Make a habit of asking, "Is Scripture being used to lift up God & point people toward Him or is it being used selfishly to control or even avoid God?"

TEACHING FOR THE LARGE GROUP: Share the "So What?" teaching with your students. You may modify it to meet your needs.

Be sure to highlight the underlined information, which gives answers to the *Student Book* questions and fill-in-the-blanks (shown in your margins).

Miles of Information!

We live in an age of information overload. In a large bookstore you'll find books on every imaginable subject from *Green Eggs and Ham* to *Bible Studies for Left-Handed Truck Drivers named Tex*. Have you visited a public library lately? There are stacks and stacks of books, rows of computers, and dozens of listening stations. The largest library of them all, the Library of Congress in Washington D.C., fills up over 530 miles of bookshelves! We have more information available to us in the Sunday paper than most people during the Middle Ages had access to in their entire lifetime. Of course, most of us now prefer the instant access of the World Wide Web where we can "Google®" any subject and find endless streams of information (and misinformation) about anything. In such a flood of information, where do we begin to find truth?

Year after year, one book remains the best seller: the Bible. No book is more widely distributed, read, and examined. Of course, no book is as widely abused, misused, and ignored than the Bible, either. Many people have Bibles and don't read them, and many who actually read them have a hard time understanding them. It is difficult to know where to begin with a book that at first glance seems to strand us in "a long time ago in a galaxy far, far away." Does this book really still matter in the twenty-first century?

The Breath of God

An important key to why we who follow Jesus hold the Bible as a central part of our faith is the belief that the Bible is "inspired." ❶ <u>The word "inspired" in the original language of the New Testament refers to the idea of "taking in breath," and the Bible itself calls the Scriptures "God-breathed"</u> (2 Timothy 3:16 NIV) and "useful" for training us to be more like Jesus. It is literally the breath of life from God to us.

❶ What does the word "inspired" mean in the original language of the New Testament?

It's important to understand that "inspiration" the way the Bible uses it goes way beyond our culture's idea of inspiration that motivates us to create, write, compose, or reach out. While many artists can reach beyond normal human ability to touch people's emotions, only ❷ <u>the "inspiration" of Scripture carries with it the authority of the word of God Himself</u>. In the Bible, God speaks above human time and culture to say things that are eternally true—true at all times in all places. In the Bible, we consistently find patterns and themes that God has woven into the fabric of our existence and that are true in any culture, place, and time. This important idea is known as "<u>revelation</u>." Since the rebellion of Adam and Eve, mankind can't see clearly anymore because our insight is distorted by our tendency toward disobedience. ❷ <u>We need help knowing what is true and what is not, and God reveals this truth to us in the Bible</u>. In fact, this truth is woven so consistently throughout the 66 books of the Old and New Testaments that we can even declare that ❷ <u>the Bible is "infallible," (truth without any mixture of error), since it tells the same story and is internally consistent with its own teaching from beginning to end</u>.

❷ What importance does each of these words used to describe the Bible carry?
A) Inspiration
B) Revelation
C) Infallible

These attributes make the Bible more than just a book. It's a sacred document that one pastor notes is "like a pool in which both children can play and elephants can swim." Millions of people go to it daily and find instruction, encouragement, and direction for living. Its depths can be explored for a lifetime. The trouble is that we are often content to either stay in the shallow end of the pool or treat Bible study as purely an academic exercise without any real application to the way we live. Jesus avoids both of these ditches. Today we'll see how He used Scripture in His life.

Learning from the Bible

Learning from the Bible ...

Matthew 4:1-11

Ask for three volunteers to come to the front and read the parts of (1) the narrator, (2) Jesus, and (3) Devil.

[NARRATOR] ¹ Then Jesus was led up by the Spirit into the wilderness to be tempted by the Devil. ² After He had fasted 40 days and 40 nights, He was hungry. ³ Then the tempter approached Him and said,
[DEVIL] "If You are the Son of God, tell these stones to become bread."
[JESUS] ... "It is written: Man must not live on bread alone but on every word that comes from the mouth of God."
[NARRATOR] ⁵ Then the Devil took Him to the holy city, had Him stand on the pinnacle of

the temple, *6 and said to Him,*

[DEVIL] *"If You are the Son of God, throw Yourself down. For it is written: He will give His angels orders concerning you and, they will support you with their hands so that you will not strike your foot against a stone."*

[JESUS] ... *"It is also written: Do not test the Lord your God."*

[NARRATOR] *8 Again, the Devil took Him to a very high mountain and showed Him all the kingdoms of the world and their splendor. 9 And he said to Him,*

[DEVIL] *"I will give You all these things if You will fall down and worship me."*

[JESUS] ... *"Go away, Satan! For it is written: Worship the Lord your God, and serve only Him."*

[NARRATOR] *11 Then the Devil left Him, and immediately angels came and began to serve Him.*

One of the benchmarks of the reality TV trend has been the show "Survivor." While many shows have tried to copy its style and concepts, it remains one of the most captivating shows of its kind. An intriguing choice each contestant has to make is what single "luxury item" he or she will bring to the remote location. Several "tribe members" have raised eyebrows and attention by choosing to bring their Bibles. Jesus would have made a similar choice as demonstrated by this story from the beginning of his ministry. As He journeyed into the desert to fast and pray, He had the Scriptures written on His heart and mind.

We discover some powerful and surprising truths about the Bible through this struggle in the life of Jesus.

(1) Jesus focused on following God's direction for His life and lived out the truth of Scripture.

Jesus said His power for living came from "seeing what the Father is doing" and then doing it Himself. Here, at the beginning of His ministry, we see Jesus "led by the Spirit" into the desert for a period of time in order to rid His life of distractions and focus solely on what God was going to tell Him. After 30 years of living a "normal" life, Jesus would soon set out on an earthly ministry leading to His crucifixion and resurrection. Jesus had the next three years to accomplish all that God sent Him to do, and He had to be prepared in every way to meet the challenges ahead. In the same way, if we're going to discover God's plan for our lives, we need to hear clearly from Him. ❸ This passage shows that in order to stay focused on God and His mission, Jesus needed time away from the crowds and distraction. We are so addicted to noise and a busy pace of life that many of us have a hard time being still for 40 minutes, let alone for 40 days! But we too need to get away from distractions and crowds in order to focus with God.

LARGE-GROUP TIME CONTINUED: This is the meat of the teaching time. Remind students to follow along and take notes in their *Student Books*.

As you share the "So What?" information with students, make it your own. Use your natural teaching style.

Emphasize underlined information, which gives key points, answers to the *Student Book* questions or fill-in-the-blanks in the (shown in your margins).

JESUS FOCUSED ON FOLLOWING GOD'S DIRECTION FOR HIS LIFE AND LIVED OUT THE TRUTH OF SCRIPTURE.
❸ What did Jesus do to stay focused on God and His mission during this desert experience?
1) He got away from the *crowds* and *distractions*.
2) He abstained from *food*.

One of the first challenges for any follower of Jesus today is to carve out and protect regular time away from the hectic pace of life and to turn off all the distractions that keep us from hearing God. ❸ <u>Another way Jesus stay focused was by "fasting"; He abstained from food in order to empty Himself and focus completely on hearing from God</u>. Fasting is a practice that is regularly used in both the Old (Leviticus 16:29, Jeremiah 36:6) and New Testaments (Matthew 6:16-18). While you should study fasting with your minister or small-group leader before trying it yourself, you can apply the same basic concept to other areas of your life. What distractions do you need to free yourself from so you can focus on God? Maybe you need a "media fast" – abstain from TV, computers, movies, and music for a while. Maybe you need a "late night fast" – make it a priority to get some sleep so you're not too worn out to focus on your daily quiet time with God or on serving others.

(2) Jesus understood the importance of the Bible, and He had prepared Himself for this desert challenge before it arrived.

We have no record of Jesus taking anything into the desert with Him. Of course, He didn't have the Bible as we know it today. By Jesus' time, the Jews had gathered most of the Old Testament together in the temple; however, these books were not easily transported (The large scrolls of the Hebrew Bible were just not that easy to backpack with into the desert!). ❹ But <u>the Holy Scriptures were with Jesus nonetheless because he had memorized them</u>. They were in His head and heart from a lifetime of studying them. It is no accident that the only reliable story we have of Jesus' childhood finds Him at the temple at the age of 12, sitting with the teachers of the law, listening and asking questions about Scripture (Luke 2:41-52).

As Jesus "grew in wisdom and stature," studying God's Word was a profound part of His development. He continually quoted Scripture, and His command of the Old Testament and His ability to apply it to everyday situations with wisdom and power astounded the common people and the highly educated rabbis.

You need to get the Bible into your life in as many ways as possible right now, while you are young. Your life may seem busy, but you will never have any more time in your life to focus your attention and heart on the Bible than right now. Not only will this help you make wise choices about how to live now ("How can a young man keep his way pure?" David writes, "By keeping Your word." – Psalm 119:9), but it will prepare you with the truth you need for the unexpected challenges ahead. It would be great if we could "TiVo" life and press pause, run to the Bible to figure out what to do, and then press play and make the wise decision. However, life isn't like that. That's why "trying" to do the right thing is not enough. You must "train" with the focus of an athlete for the life ahead of you. If Jesus, fully human but yet fully God as well, felt it important to train Himself with the knowledge of the Bible, then shouldn't you and I make it a priority?

JESUS UNDERSTOOD THE IMPORTANCE OF THE BIBLE, AND HE HAD PREPARED HIMSELF FOR THIS DESERT CHALLENGE BEFORE IT ARRIVED.
❹ How had Jesus prepared Himself for the desert challenge?

⑤ When the Devil
attempted to distort
God's Word to use it
against Him, Jesus
responded by ...
☐ Getting angry and
telling him to "shut up"
☐ Powerfully reciting
Scripture and
clinging to its truth
☐ Praying and asking
God to make
him go away

⑥ What three things
can we do to be sure
that we're using God's
Word correctly?
1) Develop a working
knowledge of
what the Bible says.
2) Discover whether the
Scripture is being used
consistently with the
meaning it had
in *its original and
total context*.
3) Make a habit of
asking: "Is Scripture
being used to *lift up* God
and point people toward
Him or is it being used
selfishly to *control or
even avoid God*?"

Don't overlook the fact that Jesus did not use His own words to respond to Satan;
He used the words of Scripture. The Bible carries authority. When Paul talks about
spiritual armor in Ephesians, it is worth noting that the *only* offensive weapon he
tells us we have is the "sword of the Spirit, which is the God's word" (Ephesians
6:17). You can't get ready for temptation or crisis; you have to be ready.

(3) Jesus knew that the enemies of God know the Bible and distort it for their own ends.

For many people, one of the real surprises of this story is that Satan knows and
actually attempted to use Scripture against Jesus. For instance, he distorted an
important if-then statement offered in Psalm 91:11-12, which says, *"If you make
the Most High your dwelling ... then no harm will befall you ... for He will command his angels concerning you."* The Devil left out the part about making God the
"dwelling." Instead, he used the verse to tempt Jesus with the self-glorification that
would come from surviving self-inflicted damage caused by taking a 450-foot leap
from the pinnacle of the temple. Jesus, however, saw through his schemes, then
clearly and **⑤** powerfully reciting Scripture and clinging to its truth.

Has it ever occurred to you that the Devil will attempt to distort or manipulate truth
as a scheme to tempt us, distract us, or lead us in the wrong direction? Sometimes
followers of Jesus also misinterpret the Bible. **⑥** How can you be sure that someone
is using the Bible accurately? Here are three keys: 1) Develop a working knowledge
or what the Bible says. 2) Discover whether the Scripture is being used consistently
with the meaning it had in its original and total context. 3) Make a habit of asking,
"Is Scripture being used to lift up God and point people toward Him, or is it being
used selfishly to control or even avoid God?"

 Do What? *(15 MINUTES)*

Group Experience: Moment of Trust

SMALL-GROUP TIME:

NOTE: This activity is
based on trust. Be sure
to stress the importance
of communication within
each group so that no
one will get hurt. Also,
be sensitive. Don't force
participation!

In your small group, stand shoulder-to-shoulder in a very tight circle. (You'll need
at least 6-7 people for this to work. If your group is smaller than this, join with
another group). One person needs to go into the center of the circle. That person will
fold his or her arms across his or her chest and will stand as still, straight, and tall
as possible. This person's feet should be together and not move during this activity.

When the group leader says, "go," the person in the center will rigidly fall back into
the waiting arms of his or her teammates who must have their hands up in the

Ask the students to divide back into small groups and discuss the "Do What?" questions. Small-group facilitators should lead the discussions and set the model for being open and honest in responding to questions.

"ready-to-catch" position. Repeat the exercise until everyone in the group has had a chance to both catch and be caught.

1. How did you feel about trusting your group members to catch you?

2. Which of these emotions did you experience as your placed your trust in them?

☐ Fear ☐ Uncertainty ☐ Doubt ☐ Confidence
☐ Trust ☐ Excitement ☐ A little bit of everything

3. Do these emotions compare with those you experience in putting your trust in the God and the Bible? Please explain.

4. After today's lesson, where do you stand in your ability to trust God's Word?
☐ I'm not falling for this stuff.
☐ I'm not sure – I want to trust the Bible, but I want to know more.
☐ I'm nervous, but I trust in God's Word.
☐ I'm plunging in – I'm ready to believe it all.

If you doubt the Bible's authenticity or are really struggling to trust it as God's Word, make plans to meet with your pastor or small-group leader soon. He or she will listen and help to answer your fears and doubts.

 # LifePoint Review

Small-group facilitators should reinforce the LifePoint for this session, make sure that student's questions are invited and addressed honestly.

The Bible is more than a just an ancient book; its message, written by men under the inspiration of God, is alive and relevant today.

"Do" Points:

These "Do" Points will help you realize this week's LifePoint. It's okay to be open and honest about your doubts as you answer the questions within your small group.

1. <u>Train yourself to make Bible study a consistent habit.</u> It's not enough to "try" Bible study. Like world-class athletes, we have to "train" ourselves to spend time with God and in His instruction manual for life in order to get its truth into our lives. **What do you need to change to make studying the Bible a priority?**

2. <u>Commit to studying the Bible in community with other Christ-followers.</u> Studying what God's has to say to us in community allows us to ask questions, to help others on the journey, and to learn from those who have been faithfully reading and learning from their Bibles for years. **What steps can you take to build or find a Bible study group?**

3. <u>Memorize portions of the Bible to get God's truth into your life.</u> Instead of seeing Bible memorization as a boring task, find creative ways to get the Bible into your head and heart. Write key verses on notecards and place them where you will see them often (on your mirror or on your car's dash). Or make a game out of memorizing a verse each week. **Can you recite a favorite Bible passage? If so, share it with the group. If not, make it your goal to memorize Psalm 119:9 or John 3:16 before next week's session.**

Prayer Connection:

This is the time to encourage, support, and pray for each other in our journeys to grasp the Bible's power and relevance in our lives.

Share prayer needs with the group, especially those related to trusting the Bible as God's Word. Your group facilitator will close your time in prayer.

Prayer Needs:

Be sure to end your session by asking students to share prayer needs with one another, especially as they relate to issues brought up by today's session.

Encourage students to list prayer needs for others in their books so they can pray for one another during the week. Assign a student coordinator in each small group to gather the group's requests and e-mail them to the group members.

Encourage students to dig a little deeper by completing a "Now What?" assignment before the next time you meet. Remind students about the "Get Ready" short daily Bible readings and related questions at the beginning of Session 5.

Remind them they are loved as they face struggles this week!

 # now What?

Deepen your understanding of who God is and continue the journey you've begun today by choosing one of the following assignments to complete this week:

Option #1:

Drive to or find a quiet place where you can "see" the farthest. Reread Matthew 4:1-11, and imagine what it must have felt like for Jesus to be out by Himself, hungry and fiercely tempted by Satan. What would you do if you were offered all that you could see for just bowing, even for a moment, to the Devil? What if you were offered your greatest dreams? Would it be tempting to accept? How would you respond? What would you say?

Option #2:

Locate Clarence Jordan's book, *The Cotton Patch Gospels* at your church or local library. Jordan was a preacher in rural Georgia during the 40's and 50's. He used his mastery of biblical Greek and translated much of the New Testament into "modern day language and places." In his book, for instance, Jesus is born in Athens, Georgia, and the Good Samaritan story takes place on the highway to Atlanta. He also applies first century truths to the issues of his era and directly discusses racism and social justice.

Taking a cue from his inspiration, translate a passage of the New Testament for your friends in your town. What issues would you address? Plan to share your letter with your small group.

Bible Reference Notes

Use these notes to deepen your understanding as you study the Bible on your own:

Matthew 4:1-11

4:1 led up by the Spirit into the wilderness to be tempted. Jesus' victory over temptation would demonstrate three things: His sinless character; an example of endurance through times of testing; and how to use Scripture as a means of defense against the devil and a support in the face of evil.

4:2 40 days. Moses fasted 40 days on Mount Sinai while receiving the commandments (Ex. 34:28), and Israel was in the wilderness 40 years (Deut. 8:2).

4:3 the tempter approached. The Spirit led Jesus into the wilderness, but it was Satan who tested Him. His challenges to Jesus came only after Jesus had entered a condition of physical weakness because of His fast. **If You are the Son of God.** This was a temptation to verify the truth of what God had declared (3:17). **bread.** Certainly it would be legitimate to turn stones to bread. Satan seemed to be inviting God's own Son to do what God did when He supplied manna to the hungry Israelites. If Jesus had used His power in this way, He would have missed accepting the experience and pain of humans, who do not have such power at their disposal.

4:4 It is written. Jesus' response is drawn from Deuteronomy 8:3. Originally this was a reflection on the meaning of the manna in the desert. True life involves not just the physical, but also the spiritual (which the Word of God feeds). Jesus will not heed Satan, but listens only to His Father, God.

4:5 temple. The second temptation takes place at the temple, which is the focal point in Israel of God's love and power. The Devil's challenge for Jesus is to prove this love and power of God by creating a peril from which God alone can rescue Him.

4:6 If You are the Son of God. Once again the challenge to Jesus is to demonstrate that He is the Messiah. **it is written.** The Devil now quotes Scripture, but does so in a way that tears it from its context. Psalm 91:11-12 are words of assurance to God's people that they can trust God to be with them even through difficult times. The Devil twists this to mean that Jesus ought to deliberately put Himself in a life-threatening situation to see if God really will bail Him out.

4:7 It is also written. Jesus responds that people are not to test God, as Deuteronomy 6:16 clearly states, but to trust Him.

4:8-9 I will give You. The final temptation has to do with gaining the kingdoms of the world without suffering the coming agonies of the cross.

4:10 it is written. Jesus draws again for the Scriptures, quoting Deuteronomy 6:13 to affirm His allegiance to God and to reject the Devil's offer.

4:11 angels came and began to serve Him. One function of angels is to bring comfort and aid to God's people just as they did for Jesus (Heb. 1:14). Thus prepared by His baptism and temptation, Jesus begins His ministry.

Psalm 91:9-13

91:3 hunter's net. The net depicted danger from any enemy. "Refuge" and "fortress" (v. 2), present the opposite image for God, making it clear that security resides only in a right relationship with Him.

91:5 terror. Terror at night is repeated in verse 6 as a plague. The arrows that fly by day indicated warfare. Whether the threats come from enemies or plague, God is our security.

91:12 against a stone. God constantly watches over His people, sending angels to guard and protect them even from common mishaps. This does not mean believers won't ever have difficulties; instead, it reminds us of God's constant awareness and concern for us.

91:13 lion ... cobra ... young lion ... serpent. Lions, cobras, and snakes are common in the Middle East and posed an unpredictable and deadly threat to people. God is not unaware of attack and can protect us.

Session

5

JESUS: PROPHET, PRIEST, KING, OR HOMEBOY?

Connections Prep

MAIN LIFEPOINT: Jesus is not just a popular religious leader; He is fully God and fully man. Jesus came as a Prophet, Priest, and King to rescue us and restore our relationship with God.

To reinforce the LifePoint, leaders and small-group facilitators should understand the following more detailed CheckPoints and "Do" Points.

BIBLE STUDY CHECKPOINTS:
- Develop an understanding of who Jesus really is
- Understand the unique relationship between God the Father and Jesus
- Reflect on the huge role Jesus plays in rescuing people from sin and death

LIFE CHANGE "DO" POINTS:
- Acknowledge our need for Jesus
- Take the first step in a lifelong commitment to following Jesus
- Commit to a lifestyle of putting Jesus first

PREPARATION:
- [ ] Review the *Leader's Book* for this session and prepare your teaching.
- [ ] Option 2: Enlist students IN ADVANCE to plan, film, edit, and show video clips of people "on the street" answering the question: "Who do you say Jesus is?"
- [ ] Option 2: Set up the TV/DVD or video system IF you choose the "Man on the Street Interviews" group experience.
- [ ] Recruit mature students or adults as small-group facilitators. Be sure these facilitators plan to attend.
- [ ] Bookmark the reading selection from C.S. Lewis' *The Lion, The Witch, and The Wardrobe* needed for the "Do What?" section.

REQUIRED SUPPLIES:
- [ ] *Essential Truth: Inviting Christ into My Reality* Leader books for each group facilitator
- [ ] *Essential Truth: Inviting Christ into My Reality* Student books for each student
- [ ] Pens or pencils for each student
- [ ] Option 1: Markers and tear sheets or poster board for each small group IF you choose the ""Jesus of the Week"" group experience
- [ ] A Copy of C.S. Lewis' book *The Lion, The Witch, and The Wardrobe*

61

Get Ready

Read one of these short Bible passages each day, and spend a few minutes discovering who the real Jesus is. Be sure to write down what's revealed to you.

MONDAY

Read John 8:48-56

Just as some people today have a hard time knowing what to do with the person of Jesus, people also had trouble understanding Jesus in His own time. What did the Jews in these verses accuse Jesus of being? What are some of the ways people "label" Jesus today?

TUESDAY

Read John 8:56-59

Jesus' claim that He existed before Abraham infuriated the Jews. Why would Jesus say such a thing if He knew it would make them mad? Do you stand up for the things you believe in, or do you say only what you think other people want to hear?

WEDNESDAY

Read John 9:13-17

Jesus was always living according to His convictions, despite the social norms of the day. What does this story tell you about what Jesus valued most?

THURSDAY

Read John 9:35-41

Jesus often reached out to and identified with the poor, the outsiders, and the social outcasts. Do you follow Jesus' example by reaching out to those who don't quite fit in? How so?

FRIDAY

Read John 12:12-19

Jesus was always careful not to draw attention to Himself. Until this point in the Gospels, He was hesitant to allow people to treat Him like a king. Why do you think Jesus entered the city of Jerusalem this way? How did His disciples react to the entry? Do you ever "miss" what God is doing right in front of you?

SATURDAY

Read Matthew 16:13-15

People haven't agreed about Jesus' identity since His time on this earth. Why do you think the people in this passage identified Him with the great prophets of Israel's past? Why was this understanding of who Jesus is not enough?

5

SUNDAY

Read Matthew 16:16-17

Jesus is often treated as a joke in modern culture. How did Peter discover who Jesus really was? Who do you say He is ... really?

LARGE-GROUP OPENING:
Get everyone's attention. Make announcements. Open your session with a prayer. Read the LifePoint to the students.

 LifePoint

Jesus is not just a popular religious leader; He is fully God and fully man. Jesus came as a Prophet, Priest, and King to rescue us and restore our relationship with God.

 # Say What? *(15 MINUTES)*

Random Question of the Week:

If police arrest a mime, should they still tell him he has the right to remain silent?

Group Experience Option #1: Jesus of the Week

The point of this exercise is to show there are many different ideas and opinions about Jesus in our culture. If time allows, visit www.jesusoftheweek.com to look for ideas to add to those the students will present. (**Warning**: do not look to this site if you are easily offended. Remember, the secular world's view of Jesus is often disrespectful and uninformed.)

- A personal list of places and ways that modern, secular culture portrays Jesus (some of these may come from Web sites, others from personal observations)
- Markers and a tear sheet or poster board

Remind the students that people outside the church, and sometimes within it, often have a distorted view of who Jesus is. He's sometimes represented as a scatter-brained cartoon prophet on comedy shows. He's portrayed as a dead and forever conquered radical on some tee-shirts. Ask the students to collectively brainstorm ways they've seen Jesus portrayed and then write them on their poster or tear sheet. Ideas may include Jesus as a religious icon or statue, as a piece of artwork, as a trouble maker, or as a prophet of peace. They may also list unusual places where they've seen images of Jesus used to make a political or social statement.

After allowing a few minutes for brainstorming, discuss the following:

1. Society often labels Jesus a "religious fanatic" or a "wild-eyed prophet." Why might people accept such stereotypes as accurate portrayals of the Son of God?

2. Considering the variety of images and ideas about Jesus that surround us, how can we discern which pictures and ideas are closest to the true Jesus?

3. Of the ideas and images listed on our tear sheet or poster, which ones stray the farthest from what the Bible teaches about Jesus? How so?

Group Experience Option #2: Man on the Street Interviews

Students love technology, ownership, and the opportunity to be creative. Enlist several of your students IN ADVANCE to plan, film, edit, and show video clips of people "on the street" answering the central question of the lesson: "Who do you say Jesus is?" If you have enough interested students with access to video cameras, every small group can put together their own. If not, several groups could film and a few students could edit all of the videos together into one longer segment.

After showing the video, discuss the following questions in small groups:

1. What was it like to interview people about Jesus? How did most people react? Were there any opportunities opened or closed to you after just mentioning the name "Jesus?"

2. What was the general consensus about who Jesus is? Why do you think there is such a wide array of opinions about this man who lived over 2,000 years ago?

3. Do you think people are interested in Jesus? What kind of Jesus are they looking for? How do you think Jesus would reach out to the people that were interviewed?

5

LARGE-GROUP TIME: Have the students turn to face the front for this teaching time. Be sure you can make eye contact with each student in the room. Encourage students to follow along and take notes in their *Student Books*.

So What? *(30 MINUTES)*

Teaching Outline

I. Who is Jesus ... really?

   A. Just about everybody's into Jesus & they all define Him however they see fit

   B. The central question is not "Who do people think Jesus is?" It's "Who do you think Jesus is?"

   C. The Bible is the only source to find the truth vs. opinion

II. Knowing who He is

   A. Difference between "knowing about" someone & actually "knowing" him

   B. In Jesus' day many thought He was a reincarnated prophet or spokesman for God

   C. God revealed the truth to Peter (Matthew 16:16-17)

   D. Jesus is more than fully man; He is also fully God

   E. Jesus was the Ultimate Prophet: He spoke absolute truth as God Himself

III. Why it matters
   A. Peter & Jesus Himself affirmed that He is the long-awaited Messiah, the Christ, the "anointed one" sent by God to rescue humanity

   B. Jesus didn't fit the popular view of His day of what the Messiah would be like

   C. Peter's declaration positioned Jesus as the One—the only One—who could rescue us from sin & death

   D. Jesus was the exact representation of God the Father because Jesus & the Father are one (John 10:30)

TEACHING FOR THE LARGE GROUP: Share the "So What?" teaching with your students. You may modify it to meet your needs.

Be sure to highlight the underlined information, which gives answers to the *Student Book* questions and fill-in-the-blanks (shown in your margins).

❶ The freethinking system prized by western culture has left everyone free to understand Jesus ...
   ☐ Just as He is
   ☐ As a prophet
   ☐ In whatever way they see fit

❷ What is the central question of life?

❸ What's one place we can turn for truth about who Jesus is?

And the Question Is ...

It's official! Jesus Christ is more famous than anyone, even The Beatles and Elvis. In the past century, the church has sought to present a more personal Jesus, making Him the most accessible personality on the planet. His image can turn up on a Sunday School classroom wall, on a trucker's belt buckle, and on a t-shirt that declares "Jesus is my Homeboy." Everyone from Billy Graham to Jessica Simpson celebrates Jesus. Almost every movement and religious ideology out there embraces his importance. Muslims, Jews, Mormons, Buddhists, evangelical right-wingers, and gay-rights advocates all have their own versions of this revolutionary rabbi. The "Jesus craze" is in full swing. ❶ Unfortunately, the freethinking system prized by western culture has left everyone free to understand Jesus in whatever way they see fit: right or wrong, flattering or otherwise.

While traveling with His disciples, Jesus asked a question that is as relevant to today's culture as it was to His, "Who do people say the Son of Man [Jesus] is?" The disciples offered several responses, proving that Jesus had many labels even early in His ministry. Some people thought He was a prophet. Some thought He was the reincarnation of someone long dead.

❷ The central question of life is: "Who do you say Jesus is? Who is He really?" As we discussed last week, anytime that issues are up for debate, we need an objective source of truth to help us out. Let's examine what ❸ the Bible—the one place we can look for the truth of Jesus' identity—says about how the disciples responded to Jesus' question.

Learning from
the Bible ...

Matthew 16:13-17

You may read the
passage yourself or
ask a volunteer to
come to the front of
the room and read it.

LARGE-GROUP TIME
CONTINUED:
This is the meat of the
teaching time. Remind
students to follow along
and take notes in their
Student Books.

As you share the
"So What?" information
with students, make
it your own. Use your
natural teaching style.

KNOWING WHO HE IS
❹ Jesus is more than
fully man; He is also
fully *God*.

Learning from the Bible

[13] *When Jesus came to region of Caesarea Philippi, He asked His disciples, "Who do people say that the Son of Man [this is a name Jesus often used of Himself] is?"* [14] *And they said, "Some say John the Baptist; others, Elijah; still others, Jeremiah or one of the prophets.* [15] *"But you," He asked them, "who do you say that I am?"* [16] *Simon Peter answered, "You are the Messiah [i.e. the Christ; the anointed one], the Son of the living God."* [17] *And Jesus responded, "Blessed are you, Simon son of Jonah, because flesh and blood did not reveal this to you, but My Father in heaven."*

Knowing Who He Is

There is a world of difference between "knowing about" someone and truly "knowing" him. For instance, we might say that we "know" a famous celebrity or sports figure, but if we do not have a relationship with them, we don't truly "know" them—we just know about them. If you are going to trust your life and your eternity to Jesus Christ, He should be more to you than just a casual acquaintance you know from a distance. When it comes to Jesus, you should be sure that He is everything He says He is. The Bible contains testimonies of dozens of men and women who knew Him, lived alongside Him, and became convinced that He was more than just an ordinary man. ❹ They claimed repeatedly that while Jesus was fully man (Hebrews 4:15), He was also fully God (John 1:14).

After more than two years of "doing life together" with His followers, Jesus wanted to know if the disciples really understood who He is or if they were as confused as the rest of the general population was about Him. Jesus launched into a critical discussion with His closest friends by posing an intentional question: "Who do *others* say that I am?" It is important that we do not discount the responses of the disciples here because they are significant. In this point in history, John the Baptist was the most outstanding religious figure to have come along. His impassioned preaching grabbed the attention of a people starved for a message of hope from God and drew the attention of the Jewish religious leaders who traveled to the desert to hear him (Matthew 3:7-10). By this point, John the Baptist had been executed by Herod (Mark 6:14-29), but his ministry had led many to believe that he was a prophet in the tradition of the Old Testament prophets who served as spokesmen for God. A common belief of the day was that great persons might be brought back to life in the form of another person. For instance, many people previously thought that John the Baptist was the prophet Elijah born again (John 1:21). Many people, Herod the King included (Mark 6:14-16), thought that Jesus was John the Baptist risen from the dead. While this was not the case, it is easy to see how this reasoning might help explain the unusual power of the carpenter from Nazareth.

Naturally, people also assumed that Jesus was Elijah, since he was one of the greatest of the prophets. Like Jesus, Elijah had raised someone from the dead (1 Kings 17:17-24). Even the prophet Malachi had prophesied that Elijah would someday return to earth, "before the great and awesome Day of the Lord comes" (Malachi 4: 5-6). So, the disciples were passing along the great respect the people had for Jesus when they said He was like John the Baptist, Elijah, Jeremiah, or "one of the prophets." While they were repeating what they had heard, they were at the same time affirming one of the characteristics of the coming Messiah. One of the "offices" (or positions of importance) held in ancient Israel was that of "prophet." ❺ If Jesus was truly the chosen One, then He would be the Ultimate Prophet who would speak absolute truth as God Himself.

❺ Jesus was the Ultimate Prophet. He spoke absolute *truth* as God *Himself*.

Why It Matters

The real heart of the issue presented in today's story is not what others said about Jesus. The central question Jesus poses to His followers is, "Who do you say that I am?" Peter's response ("You are the Messiah, the Son of the living God") is incredibly significant for at least two reasons.

**WHY IT MATTERS
❻ Why was Peter's response to Jesus' question so significant?
1) _____
2) _____**

❻ First, Peter noted that Jesus was more than just a prophet; He was *the Messiah or the Christ.* "Christ" is the Greek form of the Hebrew word "Messiah," which means "anointed one." For centuries, the Jews had awaited the arrival of this "One" who would fulfill all three Old Testament offices perfectly and reign as the perfect Prophet, Priest, and King. Nationalistic expectations had also been attached to this coming leader as well. The Messiah was expected to restore the nation of Israel to its previous splendor and set it free from Roman rule. While there were many prophets, priests, and kings in Israel's history, there would only be one Messiah. Peter's declaration that Jesus was the "One" was the opposite of what most of the Jews of the day thought. They had concluded that Jesus could not be the Messiah because He denounced violence (John 18:36) and refused to be a political leader. He chose instead to focus on the "kingdom of God" (Matthew 28:19-20).

❻ Second, Peter declared Jesus truly was the "Son of God." This belief moved the concept of Messiah beyond an ultimate earthly ruler and positioned Him as the only One who could rescue mankind from sin and death. If Jesus was the true Son of God, He was not tainted by the sin. He could die as a perfect offering for the sins of imperfect people. If Peter's assertion about Jesus was accurate, then Jesus was no mere man; He was the central figure in all of history. In fact, the Gospels record two instances in which God Himself affirmed Peter's confession. At Jesus' baptism, the voice of God said, "This is My beloved Son I take delight in Him!" (Matthew 3:17). During the "transfiguration," when a bright cloud enveloped Jesus on a mountain, God repeated His affirmation of Jesus (Matthew 17:5). So, Jesus was not merely a

❼ How could Jesus perfectly imitate or fully represent the character of God?

"son of the gods" as Roman rulers of the time claimed to be. Rather, Jesus was God's unique Son—His "one and only" (John 3:16). And as the Son of God, Jesus was the exact representation of His Heavenly Father (Hebrews 1:3). ❼ <u>Jesus perfectly imitated Him because Jesus and God were one (John 10:30)</u>.

Is That Your Final Answer?

While it may seem that the people of His day were complimenting Jesus by calling Him a great man and a prophet, the true identity of Jesus was far greater than they could imagine. Today we live in a world that is anxious to embrace Jesus. However, people are only interested in the aspects of His personality or teachings that fit within their ideology and affirm their positions. We should not make the same mistake in our time that many made when Jesus came to earth. ❽ <u>To limit Jesus in any way is to not truly understand who He is: fully man and fully God</u>. Any position or understanding of Jesus that is less than the bold but true declaration *"the Messiah, the Son of the Living God,"* denies Jesus the power to be the Savior in our everyday lives. As atheist-turned-believer Oxford scholar C.S. Lewis declared in his book *Mere Christianity*, "There is no patronizing nonsense about Jesus Christ being just a good moral teacher. Either this man was, and is, the Son of God, or else He is a madman or something worse. You can choose to spit at Him, shut Him up, and kill Him as a demon, or you can fall at His feet and call Him Lord and Savior. He did not leave any other options available to us. He did not intend to."[1]

IS THAT YOUR FINAL ANSWER?
❽ To limit Jesus in any way is ...
☐ To not truly understand who He is
☐ To degrade Him to a good, moral teacher
☐ To kill Him again

Do What? *(15 MINUTES)*

Read the segment of the story to the larger group from *The Lion, the Witch and the Wardrobe* by C.S. Lewis.

Then, break into **SMALL-GROUP TIME:** Use this time to help students begin to integrate the truth they've learned into their lives while they connect with the other students in the group, the leaders, and with God.

Group Experience: But Is He Safe?

Find a copy of *The Lion, the Witch and the Wardrobe* by C.S. Lewis: the second book in the "Chronicles of Narnia" series. This book has recently been re-published by Harper Collins (2005), and this passage begins on page 80 in this version. In the book, Aslan, the Great Lion, is the author's powerful depiction of Jesus Christ. In this section, four children have wandered through a wardrobe into the mysterious world of Narnia and are visiting with two friendly inhabitants of that world, Mr. and Mrs. Beaver. The Beavers are describing the great King, Aslan, to them.

Begin reading at the line, "an old rhyme in these parts, *Wrong will be right, when Aslan comes in sight*" and conclude with Peter's response, "I'm longing to see him ... even if I do feel frightened when it comes to the point." Focus on Mr. Beaver's assertion about Aslan, "Who said anything about safe? 'Course he isn't safe. But he's good. He's the King, I tell you."

SMALL-GROUP TIME:
Small-group facilitators should lead the discussions and encourage openness and honesty by the way they respond to the questions.

1. Why do you think C.S. Lewis chose a lion to represent Jesus? Based on today's Scripture passage, what image would you choose to represent the Jesus you see in Bible? Why?

2. How does Lewis' depiction of Jesus differ from the "meek and mild" version of Jesus that many of us have grown up with in our minds? Which is correct? How can we be sure that the Jesus we know is the real Jesus?

3. It's interesting that Lewis has his characters note that Aslan isn't "safe," but that he's "good." Do you agree with his belief that Christ is not safe, but that He is good? What do you think it means to say that Jesus isn't safe? In what ways have we tried to make Jesus and Christianity a "safe" religion? Why is it not?

 # LifePoint Review

Small-group facilitators should reinforce the LifePoint for this session. Make sure that student's questions are invited and addressed honestly.

Jesus is not just a popular religious leader; He is fully God and fully man. Jesus came as a Prophet, Priest, and King to rescue us and restore our relationship with God.

"Do" Points:

These "Do" Points will give you a handle on week's LifePoint. Be open and honest as you answer the questions within your small group.

1. Acknowledge your need for Jesus. The great lie is that somehow we can make it through this life on our own. At some point, all of us realize that life's broken; we're messed up, and we can't get to where we need to be in our own power. That's why we need a Savior—a Rescuer. If you're overwhelmed with this reality then you are close to where you need to be.
   What circumstances in your life point to your need for Jesus?

2. Take the first step in a life-long commitment to following Him. The Apostle Paul said that if we'll confess with our mouths that Jesus is Lord and believe in our hearts that God raised Him from the dead, we will be saved (see Romans 10:9). **Briefly share with the group the story of why and how you decided to accept Jesus as your Savior. If you are uncomfortable sharing, "pass" on your turn.** (Be sure to speak with your group leader right away if you have not made the decision to live for Jesus. Seek his or her guidance in making the right decision.)

3. <u>Commit to a lifestyle of putting Jesus first in your life.</u> A commitment to Jesus is requires an inward change (Romans 12:1-2). When we commit our lives to Him, we are literally transformed by the life of Jesus and given a new heart. Our relationship with Him should affect all that we do. **Have you ever wanted to do something but decided against it because it conflicted with your relationship with Jesus? Would you like to share this story with the group?**

Prayer Connection:

This is the time to encourage, support, and pray for each other in our journeys to discover who Jesus really is and how much He cares for each of us. Share prayer needs with the group, especially those related to knowing and connecting with Jesus. Your group facilitator will close your time in prayer.

Prayer Needs:

5

Be sure to end your session by asking students to share prayer needs with one another, especially as they relate to issues brought up by today's session.

Encourage students to list prayer needs for others in their books so they can pray for one another during the week. Assign a student coordinator in each small group to gather the group's requests and e-mail them to the group members.

Encourage students to dig a little deeper by completing a "Now What?" assignment before the next time you meet. Remind students about the "Get Ready" short daily Bible readings and related questions at the beginning of Session 6.

Remind them that Jesus is not safe ... but He is good!

now What?

Deepen your understanding of who Jesus is and continue the journey you've begun today by choosing one of the following assignments to complete this week:

Option #1:
Make note in your journal of all the ways you see the image of Jesus depicted or how you hear His name used. Reflect on how many different ways the name and image of Jesus are used and abused in our world. Study the life of Jesus from the Bible (Mark, Luke, Matthew, or John) so you'll be able to figure what honors Him and what falls short of the truth. Pray and prepare for opportunities to share the "real Jesus" with others.

Option #2:

Get a group of your friends together at a coffee shop or local hangout. Spend the first few minutes brainstorming questions or issues that people have concerning Jesus. Then spend the remainder of the time discussing those issues. Be careful to not build cases based on opinion. Challenge friends to use the Bible to back up their arguments. This can be excellent preparation for addressing your friends' questions about Jesus.

Bible Reference notes

Use these notes to deepen your understanding as you study the Bible on your own:

Matthew 16:13-20

16:13 Caesarea Philippi. A beautiful city on the slopes of Mount Hermon, 25 miles north of Bethsaida. It had once been called Balinas when it was a center for Baal worship. It was later called Paneas because it was said that the god Pan had his birth in a nearby cave. This region was also the headwater for the Jordan River. At the time of Jesus, it was the location of a temple dedicated to the godhead of Caesar. *Son of Man.* This is the title Jesus used most frequently for Himself. Daniel 7:13 and following provides the title's background. The Son of Man is the one invested with divine authority to rule the earth, but it was not a commonly used term for the Messiah is Jesus' day. He may have used it precisely because it did not invoke the narrowly nationalistic stereotypes of other titles.

16:14 John ... Elijah ... Jeremiah. There was a popular belief that prior to the coming of the Messiah, God would raise up Israel's famous prophets to prepare the way. Many people assumed this was the role played by Jesus.

16:15 who do you say that I am? Ultimately Jesus calls us to get beyond the opinions of others and make a decision for ourselves concerning who He is.

16:16 You are the Messiah. Peter identifies him not as the forerunner of the Christ (the Greek word for "Messiah"), but as the Messiah Himself.

16:17 flesh and blood did not reveal this to you. Jesus told the disciples that it was not by reason that people came to faith, but rather it was by revelation. The Father granted knowledge or revelation to the seeker (John 6:65). Peter responded in belief in Jesus as the Messiah (John 6:68-69).

16:18 Peter. Peter (a nickname meaning "rock"), by way of his confession, articulates the central truth, forming the foundation upon which the new people of God will be built.

16:19 keys of the kingdom of heaven. This is an allusion to Isaiah 22:15-24 in which God declared that he would give the "key to the house of David" to a new steward who would replace the old one who had been irresponsible.

John 8:48-59

8:41 your father. Having denied that they are Abraham's children in verse 40, Jesus' statement here raises the question of whose children they really are. *We weren't born of sexual immorality.* The crowd was probably referring to the irregular circumstances behind Jesus' birth.

8:59 they picked up stones. Stoning was the punishment for blasphemy against "the name of the LORD" (Lev. 24:16). The incredulity and scorn of verses 52 and 57 turns to fury at Jesus' bold assertion in 58.

John 12:12-13

12:12 the large crowd. This was obviously a very large crowd of Jews in town for the Passover. Jerusalem was a city of normally under 25,000 people. When Passover was celebrated, the population increased to 4 or 5 times its normal size.

12:13 palm branches. The other Gospels, in telling this story, mention people using their garments as well. *Hosanna!* Originally a one word prayer for God to save (Ps. 118:25), this had become an expression of praise. *Blessed is He who comes in the name of the Lord.* Psalm 118:26 was used in the liturgy for Passover and celebrated God's deliverance of Israel from her enemies.

1 C.S. Lewis, *Mere Christianity* (San Francisco: Harper, 2001.)

Session

6

BREAKING THE BOND: CAN I BE FREE?

Connections Prep

MAIN LIFEPOINT: God loves us and wants to rescue us from the bondage and death that comes from disobeying Him and going our own way. God offers us forgiveness and a new start through Jesus Christ.

To reinforce the LifePoint, leaders and small-group facilitators should understand the following more detailed CheckPoints and "Do" Points.

BIBLE STUDY CHECKPOINTS:
· Recognize that we've all messed up and are in need of a new start
· Understand that God provides forgiveness for our failures and rebellion
· Realize the depth of God's love for us

LIFE CHANGE "DO" POINTS:
· Admit our need for forgiveness
· Confess our faith in Jesus as the One who gives us fresh starts
· Commit to extending the forgiving power of Jesus to others

PREPARATION:
☐ Review the *Leader's Book* for this session and prepare your teaching.
☐ Recruit students or adults as small-group facilitators. Be sure they attend.
☐ Option 1: Set up the TV/DVD or video system IF you choose the "We're a Bunch of Goonies" group experience. OR ... Option 2: Set up an audio system IF you choose the "Pictures of the Past" group experience.
☐ Make a wooden or paper cross to display at the head of the room for the "Do What?" segment near the end of this session. You may put candles around it

REQUIRED SUPPLIES:
☐ *Essential Truth* Leader books for each group facilitator
☐ *Essential Truth: Inviting Christ into My Reality* Student books for each student
☐ Pens or pencils for each student
☐ Option 1: Rent the movie *Goonies* IF you choose the "We're a Bunch of Goonies" group experience
☐ Option 2: Obtain Warren Barfield's song, "Pictures of the Past" IF you choose the "Pictures of the Past" experience. It's on the CD entitled, "Warren Barfield" (Creative Artists Trust, 2003). Find a way to project the lyrics if possible.
☐ 3x5 cards for each student

 **Get Ready**

Read one of these short Bible passages each day, and spend a few minutes listening to God and your heart. Be sure to journal what you're learning about freedom.

MONDAY   **Read John 3:1-3**

Nicodemus came to Jesus at night. Why do you think he chose to approach Jesus in the evening? Why do you think Jesus answered him the way He did?

TUESDAY   **Read John 3:4-7**

Birth is a complicated process and is certainly not one that we would choose to repeat. How would you have reacted to Jesus' comments about needing to be "born again?"

WEDNESDAY   **Read John 3:8-9**

Jesus compared the Holy Spirit to the wind. You can't physically see the breeze, but you can feel its effects. What does Jesus' analogy suggest about the Holy Spirit's presence and ability to influence your life?

THURSDAY   **Read John 3:10-15**

Jesus helped Nicodemus make the connection between new birth and eternal life. Why is a concept like being "born again" difficult to understand? What other Christian teachings puzzle you? Take your questions to God and wait for Him to answer.

FRIDAY

Read John 3:16-17

Many Christ-followers can recite John 3:16. Can you? How about verse 17? Is John 3:16 more important than John 3:17? Why is each verse significant?

SATURDAY

Read Romans 6:7

Sin is thoughts and behaviors that hurt us or separate us from God. Sinful behaviors such as disobedience, lies, greed, and manipulation entrap us. What specific sins try to trap you? Paul writes that we "should no longer be slaves to sin." But how exactly are we freed from it?

SUNDAY

Read Romans 6:8-11

Paul says we are alive to God. How do his words help to explain forgiveness? How important is it to understand forgiveness?

6

LARGE-GROUP OPENING:
Get everyone's attention. Make announcements. Open your session with a prayer. Read the LifePoint to the students.

 LifePoint

God loves us and wants to rescue us from the bondage and death that comes from disobeying Him and going our own way. God offers us forgiveness and a new start through Jesus Christ.

 Say What? *(15 MINUTES)*

Random Question of the Week:
Why do you think God made armadillos? Koalas? Jellyfish?

Option #1 Group Experience: We're a Bunch of Goonies

· TV/DVD or video system
· The movie *Goonies*

Remember the scene in *Goonies* where the bad guys catch the little chubby kid? They interrogate him to find out what happened to the treasure map. When they tell him to "spill your guts, kid," he starts into a true confessions time about all the bad things he did in grade school, including "... and the worst thing I ever done ..."

This scene is part of "Chunk Hitches a Ride" and begins at 51:54 minutes on the DVD; you could also show the continuation at 58:07. (Queue up this scene before your session begins.)

Discuss the following questions in your small group:

1. As a group, make a list of the "top ten most difficult things about surviving grade school" (David Letterman style). These should be pretty funny. Some things that may make the list are warm curdled milk at lunch and not getting cooties from girls.

2. If you had to confess your grade school "sins," what would you confess?

3. If you could call "do-over" and get a fresh start to your entire life that would erase all the bad things you've done and wipe out all the times you've hurt others, would you do it? Why or why not?

Option #2 Group Experience: Pictures of the Past
(Permission is granted to copy only this page for use by small-group facilitators as part of the Life Connections® Youth *Essential Truth* study.)

Sidebar:

Play the video clip from the *Goonies* for the whole group (option #1 ... OR ... play the "Pictures of the Past" song for the whole group (option #2).

Then, break into **SMALL-GROUP TIME:** Instruct students to separate into smaller groups of 4-8, preferably in a circle configuration. Call on the mature student or adult leaders you recruited to facilitate each small group through the "Say What?" segment.

· CD player
· Warren Barfield's song, "Pictures of the Past"
· Overhead projector (optional)
· Overhead transparency with the printed lyrics to "Pictures of the Past."

Play the song "Pictures of the Past" for the entire group. This tune uses a good dose of tongue-in-cheek humor and an awkward grade-school memory to discuss an important subject: forgiveness. It possible, project the song's lyrics on the wall by overhead projector. If you can't, ask the students to pay close attention to the song's words. After the song has finished playing, have the students discuss the following questions within their small groups.

Discuss the questions at the end of the Option #1 Group Exercise in your small group.

 So What? *(30 MINUTES)*

G

Teaching Outline

I. Hemingway's Story of Paco
    A. 800 guys responded
    B. Need for forgiveness is universal—something we all long for

II. The Larger Story
    A. The Great Betrayal & the Origin of Evil: Isaiah 14:12-15; Ezekiel 28:14-17
    B. The Glory of Man & the Fall into Darkness: Genesis 3; Romans 3:23
    C. The Rescue Mission: Colossians 1:13-14; 1 Corinthians 3:18
    D. The Unseen Reality: 1 Peter 5:8; 2 Corinthians 4:18

Summary: (1) There's a <u>villain</u> in the story. (2) He <u>deceived</u> humanity and caused us to fall too. (3) God has <u>rescued us</u> through Jesus. (4) The villain uses <u>lies</u> as his main tactic to keep us from God. He uses live ammunition and his attacks are <u>real</u>. (5) His goal is to cause us to doubt the <u>heart of God</u> toward us. (6) God offers to restore us, but allows <u>freedom to choose</u>, because without freedom of will, there is no love and relationship.

LARGE-GROUP TIME: Have the students turn to face the front for this teaching time. Be sure you can make eye contact with each student in the room. Encourage students to follow along and take notes in their *Student Books*.

III. The Story Behind John 3:16
A. Jesus not bothered by questions, if they're genuine and honest

B. Spiritual rebirth: experiencing forgiveness for failures and sins and the life that God offers through belief in His one and only Son

C. "Born again" best describes how we're rescued from rebellious nature of our first birth

D. We have a choice: life with Jesus or continued rebellion that leads to spiritual death

Ernest Hemingway once told the story of a Spanish father who, after years of loneliness, decided to reconcile the strained relationship he had with his son. The father placed an ad in a Madrid newspaper that read, "Paco, meet me at Hotel Montana at noon on Tuesday and all is forgiven. Love, Papa." When the father arrived at the hotel, he found 800 young men named Paco who were waiting for their fathers! ❶ What this story reveals is that the need for forgiveness is universal—something we all long for. At some point, we offend or hurt others, or, worse yet, we fail to respect God with our lifestyles and choices. At some point, we realize that our only hope is to confess that we have made a mistake and ask for a new start. What's amazing is that the Bible tells us this is possible! God, in His infinite wisdom and care, provides a way for us to be start clean.

The Larger Story
We cannot understand forgiveness unless we start grasp larger story. The larger story began before there was life on earth. It's the story that we were all born into and exist for. Without it our lives are only a meaningless series of joyful and painful events followed by death. Here's the basic story:

(1) The Great Betrayal and the Origin of Evil
Isaiah 14:12-15 and Ezekiel 28:14-17 refer to Satan, as a fallen "star" or angel who set himself up in rebellion against God and was cast out of heaven and thrown to earth. He's called the "destroyer of nations," and "will be brought down to Sheol into the deepest regions of the Pit."

(2) The Glory of Man and the Fall into Darkness
Genesis 3 says, "In the beginning ... God created man in His own image, in the image of God He created him; male and female He created them." But the Great Betrayer deceived Adam and Eve, causing them to turn away from following God. Since that fall, the Bible says, "all have sinned and fall short of the glory of God" (Romans 3:23).

(3) The Rescue Mission

God loves us deeply and through Jesus, "has rescued us from the domain of darkness and transferred us into the kingdom of the Son He loves, in whom we have redemption, the forgiveness of sins" (Colossians 1:13-14). His goal is to transform us into our former glory—the glory of Jesus (1 Corinthians 3:18).

(4) The Unseen Reality

The bad guy is still on the loose. 1 Peter 5:8 says, "Your adversary the Devil is prowling around like a roaring lion, looking for anyone he can devour." Because he is a real enemy, we're warned to focus on what is unseen, not just what we can see (2 Corinthians 4:18). His main tactic is still lying and trying to get us to doubt the goodness and heart of God.

❷ The Reader's Digest® Version:

(1) There's a villain in the story. (2) He deceived humanity and caused us to fall from God too. (3) God has rescued us through Jesus. (4) The villain uses lies as his main tactic to keep us from God. He uses live ammunition and his attacks are real. (5) His goal is to cause us to doubt the heart of God toward us. (6) God offers to restore us, but allows freedom to choose, because without freedom of will, there is no love and relationship.

Today we'll listen in on a conversation between Jesus and a member of the Jewish ruling council that helps to explain forgiveness and how we can have a new start with God.

Learning from the Bible

[NARRATOR] ¹ *There was a man from the Pharisees named Nicodemus, a ruler of the Jews.* ² *This man came to Him at night and said,*

[NICODEMUS] *"Rabbi, we know that You have come from God as a teacher, for no one could perform these signs You do unless God were with him."*

[JESUS] ³ *"I assure you: Unless someone is born again, he cannot see the kingdom of God."*

[NICODEMUS] ⁴ *"But how can anyone be born when he is old? Can he enter his mother's womb a second time and be born?"*

[JESUS] ⁵ *"I assure you: Unless someone is born of water and the Spirit, he cannot enter the kingdom of God.*

⁶ *Whatever is born of the flesh is flesh, and whatever is born of the Spirit is spirit.*

⁷ *Do not be amazed that I told you that you must be born again.*

⁸ *The wind blows where it pleases, and you hear its sound, but you don't know where it comes from or where it is going. So it is with everyone born of the Spirit."*

---

❷ THE LARGER STORY:
(1) There's a *villain* in the story.
(2) He *deceived* humanity and caused us to fall from God too.
(3) God has *rescued us* through Jesus.
(4) The villain uses *lies* as his main tactic to keep us from God. He uses live ammunition and his attacks are *real*.
(5) His goal is to cause us to doubt the *heart of God* toward us.
(6) God offers to restore us, but allows *freedom to choose*, because without freedom of will, there is no love and relationship.

Learning from the Bible …

John 3:1-17

Ask for two volunteers to come to the front and read the parts of (1) Jesus and (2) Nicodemus. You can read the part of the Narrator. Try to call on those who have not read before the class during this study.

G

[NICODEMUS] *9 "How can these things be?"*

[JESUS] *10 "Are you a teacher of Israel and don't know these things?" 11 "I assure you: We speak what We know and We testify to what We have seen, but you do not accept Our testimony.*

12 If I have told you about things that happen on earth and you don't believe, how will you believe if I tell you about things of heaven?

13 No one has ascended into heaven except the One who descended from heaven—the Son of Man.

14 Just as Moses lifted up the snake in the wilderness, so the Son of Man must be lifted up, 15 so that everyone who believes in Him will have eternal life.

16 "For God loved the world in this way: He gave His One and Only Son, so that everyone who believes in Him will not perish but have eternal life.

17 For God did not send His Son into the world that He might condemn the world, but that the world might be saved through Him.

The Story Behind John 3:16

LARGE-GROUP TIME CONTINUED:
This is the meat of the teaching time. Remind students to follow along and take notes in their *Student Books.*

As you share the "So What?" information with students, make it your own. Use your natural teaching style. You may modify it with your own perspectives and teaching needs. Emphasize the underlined information, which gives key points, answers to the *Student Book* questions or fill-in-the-blanks in the (shown in your margins).

❸ Jesus was not bothered by questions, even difficult ones, as long as they came from people who were *genuine* and *honest* in their quest to find *God.*

If you have been around the church culture at all, you have likely heard the verse John 3:16 quoted and sung and inscribed on banners, Bibles, and posters. If you've paid close attention to various sporting events, you might have even caught a glimpse of a "banner man," a passionate believer who makes a good-natured attempt to blend his love for sports and God by simply writing "JOHN 3:16" on a huge poster that he displays just before a field goal attempt is made and the TV cameras are pointed his way. So, what's the deal with this verse? Why is it so important, and what inspired Jesus to say it in the first place?

John's story of the encounter between Jesus and Nicodemus opens with several interesting details. First, he tells us that Nicodemus was a Pharisee and a member of the Jewish ruling council. He was a man of tremendous political and social power, yet he sought out an audience with Jesus. Nicodemus began the conversation by complimenting Jesus as a teacher who has "come from God." As a group the Pharisees were so threatened by Jesus that they eventually conspired to have Him killed, but Nicodemus was an honest seeker. ❸ Jesus was not bothered by questions, even difficult ones, as long as they came from people who were genuine and honest in their quest to find God.

Jesus immediately got to the heart of his visitor's question: to be a part of God's kingdom, you have to be "born again." The idea of being "born again" is as difficult for us to grasp as it must have been for Nicodemus. Words and phrases such as "born again" and "saved" have been used so casually in our church culture for so long that few truly understand what they mean anymore. A critical issue facing the church today is false teachings that attempt to "add on" to the salvation Jesus offered. For some, being "born again" means having an emotional experience. For others, it means walking an aisle and becoming a member of a certain church or denomination. But Jesus took great lengths to make sure the meaning was clear. When Nicodemus defaulted to a literal interpretation of "born again," Jesus assured him that it is not a physical rebirth He was discussing, but a spiritual one.

4 So, what is this spiritual rebirth? No one can enter the kingdom of God unless he experiences forgiveness for his failures and sins and the life that God offers through belief in His one and only Son.

4 What is spiritual rebirth?

So, why is being "born again" such an important idea? **5** Because it is how Jesus best described how we are rescued from the rebellious nature of our first birth. When we are born, we come into a world that has been broken and evil since the time of Adam and Eve. Therefore, we inherit the tendency to sin. Sin always leads to a physical death and spiritual death. This concept is sometimes called "original sin," and if you don't believe it is true, ask the parent of any young child to affirm the ability of even the youngest to lie, cheat, and manipulate. We are already "dead in sins" based on our first birth into a sinful nature. If we are going to live eternally, then we must have a "second birth" spiritually.

5 Why is the phrase "born again" so important?

6 The "second birth" happens when we accept the God-story of John 3:16-17, that God loved us so much that He did not leave us without hope but provided a rescue through His Son, Jesus. God has provided a "second chance" for us through Jesus, but this "gift of God" (eternal life) (Romans 6:23) is just that—a gift. A person still has to accept it. God will not force someone to accept Him against his or her will.

6 At what point is one "born again"?

6

Just because God doesn't want us to die in our sin doesn't mean we won't. **7** We have a choice in the matter, and we can choose to hold on to our rebellion until it drags us to our death, physically and spiritually. God desires that we believe in Jesus. "Belief" here means more than just mental assent to an idea. It means trusting that God is who He says He is and accepting that Jesus can truly forgive our failures. Even when we feel the things we've done are too horrible to ever be forgiven, we can trust God's promise that "whoever" believes in Jesus will be saved. **7** The answer to Nicodemus' question, "But how can anyone be born when he is old?" is "by the forgiveness of God that comes through faith in Jesus!"

7 How can we be "born again"? Who has the choice about our life and destiny?

Do What? *(15 MINUTES)*

Group Experience: At The Foot of The Cross

1. Read 1 John 1:8-10 silently. Then, working as a group, summarize the message.

2. On your 3x5 card, write out a specific thing you've done or said this week for which you need forgiveness. Don't worry. No one will read your card.

3. Pray silently. Confess what's on the card to God. Ask Him to forgive you, then tear up the card and scatter its pieces around the base of the cross at the front of the room. This illustrates what happens when we acknowledge our wrongdoings and accept Jesus' love and forgiveness.

4. After you've scattered the pieces, return to your circle. Take turns describing how today's session made you feel. What did you learn about forgiveness?

 # LifePoint Review

God loves us and wants to rescue us from the bondage and death that comes from disobeying Him and going our own way. God offers us forgiveness and a new start through Jesus Christ.

"Do" Points:

These "Do" Points will help you grab hold of this week's LifePoint. Be open and honest as you answer the questions within your small group.

1. Admit you need forgiveness. 1 John 1:8 says, "If we say, 'We have no sin,' we are deceiving ourselves, and the truth is not in us." Jesus had compassion for people who admitted and felt the pain of their sin, no matter how messed up they were. He condemned those who acted like they were morally perfect and not in need God's forgiveness.
Why is it important to ask for forgiveness every day?

2. <u>Confess your faith in Jesus as the one who gives you a new start.</u> Jesus doesn't just forgive our failures. He wipes them away and doesn't remember them anymore. He asks only that we tell Him our mistakes and admit our need of His help. **How can confession lead to a "new start"? Give an example of how confession has given you a fresh outlook on life.**

3. <u>Commit to extending the forgiving power of Jesus to others.</u> As a Christ-follower, forgiveness should become part of your lifestyle as you become more like Jesus. Your life should become a testimony to His incredible power to forgive. **Who hurt you this week? How can you extend forgiveness to that person?**

Prayer Connection:

This is the time to encourage, support, and pray for each other. Share prayer needs with the group, especially those related to forgiving those who have wronged you. Your group facilitator will close your time in prayer.

Prayer Needs:

Be sure to end your session by asking students to share prayer needs with one another, especially as they relate to issues brought up by today's session.

Encourage students to list prayer needs for others in their books so they can pray for one another during the week. Assign a student coordinator in each small group to gather the group's requests and e-mail them to the group members.

Encourage students to dig a little deeper by completing a "Now What?" assignment before the next time you meet. Remind students about the "Get Ready" short daily Bible readings and related questions at the beginning of Session 7.

 now What?

Deepen your understanding of who God is, and continue the journey you've begun today by choosing one of the following assignments to complete this week:

Option #1:

Take a walk with a couple of friends from your small group by a creek, pond, lake, or river. Spend time in silence thinking about and confessing your failures to God.

As you think of each failure, pick up a rock from the riverbank. As you ask forgiveness for that offense, throw the rock into the creek and remember the words of David in Psalm 103:10-12, "He has not dealt with us as our sins deserve ... as far as the east is from the west, so far has He removed our transgressions from us."

Option #2:

Use the concordance in the back of your Bible and any reference tools you have to study at least three passages that discuss the term "forgiveness." Copy each passage into your journal, recording your thoughts, feelings, and responses to it. If the Holy Spirit prompts you to apply what you're learning to a particular situation, then move forward prayerfully and powerfully.

βible Reference notes

Use these notes to deepen your understanding as you study the Bible on your own:

John 3:1-17

3:1 Pharisees. Judaism was divided into various sects along doctrinal, political, practical, and social lines. The Pharisees were committed to the principle that religious and ethical purity was the means of securing God's favor. This in turn led to a concern for the fine points of the Law, which tended to overshadow the essence of that Law. **Nicodemus.** Nicodemus, a respected religious authority (v. 10), appears also in 7:50 and 19:39 but in no other Gospel. **ruler of the Jews.** Nicodemus was a member of the Sanhedrin — the religious and political governing body of Judea. Comprised of 71 members and presided over by the high priest, its self-perpetuating membership included priests, elders, and scribes.

3:3 born again. This phrase can be translated in two ways—"born again" or "born from above." The former highlights the radical reorientation to life resulting from trusting Jesus, while the latter accents the reality that spiritual life is a gift from God, not something earned by virtue of one's performance (1:12-13).

3:5 born of water and the Spirit. Commentators differ on what is meant here: (1) Some think this phrase is a restatement of the call for a spiritual birth in addition to physical birth (v. 3); (2) Others assume water illustrates the life-giving qualities of the Spirit (7:38-39); (3) Others think that the author, writing about A.D. 90, refers to contemporary practices of water baptism as a symbol of the baptism in the Spirit.

3:13 ascended into heaven except. This Gospel's witness to Jesus is from the perspective of the whole story already told; hence the author can refer to the ascension of Jesus even at this point.

3:14 snake. Because of rebellion, God sent deadly serpents into the midst of the Israelites. When they called for mercy, God instructed Moses to put a statue of a serpent on a pole. Whoever looked upon that statue would not die (Num. 21:4-9). In a similar way, when people look with faith upon Jesus who is "lifted up" (another double-edged phrase referring both to His crucifixion and His resurrection/ascension), their judgment is averted and they are brought into life (6:40).

3:15 eternal life. This is the first use of a phrase seen repeatedly throughout this Gospel. Its meaning is not simply tied up with the quantity of time one exists, but also with the quality of fullness, goodness, and perfection of life with God.

3:16 God loved the world in this way. The great motivation behind God's plan of salvation (1 John 4:9-10). **He gave.** This is evidenced especially in the act of Jesus' life and crucifixion.

3:17 that the world might be saved through Him. The whole point of Jesus' mission was to provide all people with access to God.

Session

7

FEAR FACTOR: WHAT HAPPENS WHEN SOMEONE DIES?

Connections Prep

MAIN LIFEPOINT: God promises eternal life to those who have a personal relationship with Jesus. That assurance gives Christ-followers hope for the future and drives them to live passionately in the present.

To reinforce the LifePoint, leaders and small-group facilitators should understand the following more detailed CheckPoints and "Do" Points.

BIBLE STUDY CHECKPOINTS:
- Evaluate life by imagining death
- Acknowledge God's promise of life after death for those who believe and trust in Jesus
- Understand Jesus Christ's role in assuring us of the promise of eternal life

LIFE CHANGE "DO" POINTS:
- Personally trust in Jesus' promise of eternal life
- Learn to talk openly about death
- Commit to live passionate, "no regrets" lives

7

PREPARATION:
- ☐ Review the *Leader's Book* for this session and prepare your teaching.
- ☐ Determine how you will subdivide students into small discussion groups.
- ☐ Recruit mature students or adults as small-group facilitators. Be sure these facilitators plan to attend.

REQUIRED SUPPLIES:
- ☐ *Essential Truth: Inviting Christ into My Reality* Leader books for each group facilitator
- ☐ *Essential Truth: Inviting Christ into My Reality* Student books for each student
- ☐ Pens or pencils for each student
- ☐ Blank copy paper for each student

 Get Ready

Read one of these short Bible passages each day and spend a few minutes wrapping your brain around it. Be sure to jot down any "killer" insights.

MONDAY **Read John 11:17-22**
There are bad days and there are "rotten, horrible, hideously bad days." Mary and Martha lost their brother and the provider for their family all at once. What happened on the worst day of your life? How did those events impact the strength of your faith?

TUESDAY **Read John 11:23-27**
"Resurrections" are not everyday occurrences. But are miracles common daily events? Do you ever doubt that Jesus was really raised from the dead and had power over death? Why or why not?

WEDNESDAY **Read John 11:28-32**
It has been said that when life squeezes us, our response to the pressure explains the true value of our character. Mary was obviously "squeezed" as she grieved the loss of Lazarus. When something bad happens to you, how do you handle it? How do you feel towards others during those times?

THURSDAY **Read John 11:33-35**
Jesus was moved by the outpouring of emotion from Mary and her friends. When was the last time you were honest with Jesus over pain in your life? Be encouraged that Jesus wept very real tears over the hurt of His friends. Why did He respond that way?

FRIDAY

Read John 11:36-37

The love of Jesus was evident to observers. How do others demonstrate their love for you? Do you feel that God loves you in the same way your parents or best friends do? Explain.

SATURDAY

Read John 11:38-40

John records Lazarus' decay in morbid detail. Why is his description important? What's the most amazing thing you have ever seen God do?

SUNDAY

Read John 11:41-44

Has there ever been a time when you doubted that God could hear you? If so, why? Have you ever asked Him for something so outrageous that you wondered if and how He would respond? If God could answer any prayer for you right now, no matter how big or small, what would it be?

7

LARGE-GROUP OPENING:
Get everyone's attention. Make announcements. Open your session with a prayer. Read the LifePoint to the students.

 LifePoint

God promises eternal life to those who have a personal relationship with Jesus. That assurance gives Christ-followers hope for the future and drives them to live passionately in the present.

SMALL-GROUP TIME:
Instruct students to
separate into smaller
groups of 4-8, prefer-
ably in a circle con-
figuration. Call on the
mature student or adult
leaders you recruited
to facilitate each small
group through this "Say
What?" segment.

 # Say What? *(15 MINUTES)*

Random Question of the Week:

How would the world change if diamonds were suddenly worthless and seashells became as valuable as gold?

Group Experience: Play It Forward

· Blank copy paper for each student
· Pens or pencils

1. What would your friends or family say that you are "famous" for? Share it with the group.

2. Imagine your life as it might be 60 years from now. Visualize where you may be living, what you might be doing, and what you may have accomplished.

LEADER NOTE: After giving students a few moments to think about question #2, ask them to imagine for a moment that they have died. Point out that you are not need-lessly trying to be morbid today, but that the group needs a starting place to begin discussing a very sensitive and difficult subject. **Pass out the paper and pens.** Tell students that you want them to use their imagined information to write their own obituaries the way they want them to read someday. Obituaries are brief articles about people who have passed away. Question 3 has the list of elements to include.

3. Write out your own obituary following your leader's instructions. Include:

· The deceased's full name, birth date, and date of death

· A list of surviving family members

· Where the deceased was living at the time of his or her death

· The deceased's occupation, hobbies, interests, and greatest accomplishments

LEADER NOTE: Give the students a few minutes to write, and then ask for volun-teers to read their obituaries aloud.

After hearing one or two obituaries read, discuss the following:

88

4. In our culture, we don't think or talk about death very often. In fact, students usually avoid the topic if at all possible. Why is it difficult to talk about death?

5. Was it strange to write your own obituary? (I hope so!) How did considering your own mortality make you feel? What was your gut-level reaction to hearing the obituaries of your friends?

 So What? *(30 MINUTES)*

Teaching Outline

I. Nobel's Legacy
  A. Mistaken obituary focused on weapons & mass destruction
  B. Changed his life & now revered as namesake of Nobel Prize

II. The Burning Questions
  A. Many pretend they're only concerned with this life
  B. #1 – What happens when you die?
  C. #2 – How will I be remembered?

III. Understanding Jesus' Power Over Death
  A. Word of mouth – the powerful marketing buzz
  B. Jesus created a buzz with Lazarus' resurrection from the dead
  C. Jesus demonstrated through miracles that He is a supernatural force

IV. "Lord, if You had been here, my brother wouldn't have died"
  A. Belief that Jesus could have prevented the death
  B. Where was God? If God had really been there ..."
  C. We're all terminal – Jesus only delayed death for Lazarus
  D. Real death to be concerned about: second (spiritual) death
  E. Jesus has ultimate power over death itself

LARGE-GROUP TIME: Have the students turn to face the front for this teaching time. Be sure you can make eye contact with each student in the room. Encourage students to follow along and take notes in their *Student Books*.

Share the "So What?" information with your large group of students. You may modify it with your own perspectives and teaching needs. Be sure to highlight the underlined information, which gives answers to the *Student Book* questions and fill-in-the-blanks (shown in your margins).

V. **"I am the resurrection and the life. The one who believes in Me, even though he dies, will live. Everyone who lives and believes in Me will never die—ever."**

    A. Seems full of contradictions: "live, even though he dies" ... "everyone who lives and believes in Me will never die—ever"

    B. Two different meanings for "die" — all die physically; not all die spiritually

    C. Key: trust & hope in Jesus = resurrected to live forever with God

    D. In next life our spirits break free from weaknesses imposed on our bodies

    E. Hope & continuing spiritual life for those who believe in and follow Jesus!

VI. **"Loose him and let him go"**

    A. Lazarus' grave clothes binding & limiting

    B. Many people walking around in "grave clothes" — fearing unknown or death

    C. John 10: Satan is the thief of life, but Jesus offers more than ever dreamed

    D. Hebrews 2:14-15 (NIV)

    E. Apostle Paul (beheaded in Rome in AD 65) — "To live is Christ ... die gain"

    F. Bonhoeffer (hung in Nazi Germany in 1945 for preaching) — "This is the end. For me, the beginning of life."

    G. Missionary Jim Elliot (murdered by the tribe he was helping) — "He is no fool, he who gives that which he cannot keep to gain that which he cannot lose."

VII. **Jesus has conquered death so we can be truly free to live a life of no regrets.**

    A. Raising of Lazarus a demonstration of God's power over death

    B. An illustration of what is to come to everyone who believes in Christ

    C. Will you believe & start a never-ending life? (see verses 25, 26, and 40)

TEACHING FOR THE LARGE GROUP:
Share the "So What?" teaching with your students. You may modify it to meet your needs.

Be sure to highlight the underlined information, which gives answers to the *Student Book* questions and fill-in-the-blanks (shown in your margins)

Nobel's Legacy

Dr. Alfred Nobel was a famed chemist who lived in Sweden during the early part of the 20th century. One day Nobel was reading the morning paper when he came across a shocking obituary—his own! It seems his brother had recently died and the paper mistakenly printed the notice for Alfred. The article said Nobel would be remembered for inventing powerful explosives used to achieve new levels of mass destruction. When the shock of reading his own obituary subsided, Nobel realized that he would be remembered as a person who used his skills to bring about destruction. He wouldn't be remembered for his talents or the good he did. Immediately, Nobel began to reevaluate his life. He used his wealth to establish a fund that would reward people for acts of positive service to mankind. Today Alfred Nobel is revered worldwide as the namesake of the Nobel Prize, an award honoring courageous achievements in arts, sciences, and efforts towards world peace.

❶ Many people *pretend* that they are only concerned with this life.

❷ The burning questions that everyone wants to ask is, "What *happens* when you *die*?" and "How will I be *remembered*?"

Learning from the Bible ...

John 11:17-44

Ask for six volunteers to come to the front and read the parts of (1) the narrator, (2) Mary, (3) Martha, (4) Jesus, (5) the sympathetic Jews, and (6) the skeptical Jews.

To save time, you could also read the passage yourself.

❶ Many people pretend that they are only concerned with this life. But how does that explain the recent popularity of entertainment that addresses what happens after death? Movies and TV shows like *The Sixth Sense, What Dreams May Come, Constantine, The Five People You Meet in Heaven,* and the series *24* all explore life-and-death themes. The ever-present threat of terrorism and war, and raging natural disasters such as the tsunami that killed thousands in a few moments lead us to ❷ the burning questions that everyone wants to ask, "What happens when you die?" and "How will I be remembered?"

So how do we answer these questions? Where do we begin? Today we'll look at the story of the death and resurrection of Lazarus. This is an atypical story because it involves a physical resurrection, something that obviously doesn't happen every day. But, it's also an incredible story of hope that is significant for our era.

Learning from the Bible

[NARRATOR] [17] When Jesus arrived, He found that Lazarus had already been in the tomb four days. [18] Bethany was near Jerusalem (about two miles away). [19] Many of the Jews had come to Martha and Mary to comfort them about their brother. [20] As soon as Martha heard that Jesus was coming, she went to meet Him. But Mary remained seated in the house. [21] [MARTHA] "Lord, if You had been here, my brother wouldn't have died. [22] Yet even now I know that whatever You ask from God, God will give You."
[23] [JESUS] "Your brother will rise again."
[24] [MARTHA] "I know that he will rise again in the resurrection at the last day."
[25] [JESUS] "I am the resurrection and the life. The one who believes in Me, even if he dies, will live. [26] Everyone who lives and believes in Me will never die—ever. Do you believe this?"
[27] [MARTHA] "Yes, Lord, I believe You are the Messiah, the Son of God, who was to come into the world."
[28] [NARRATOR] Having said this, she went back and called her sister Mary, saying in private, [MARTHA] "The Teacher is here and is calling for you."
[29] [NARRATOR] As soon as she heard this, she got up quickly and went to Him. [30] Jesus had not yet come into the village but was still in the place where Martha had met Him. [31] The Jews who were with her in the house consoling her saw that Mary got up quickly and went out. So they followed her, supposing that she was going to the tomb to cry there. [32] When Mary came to where Jesus was and saw Him, she fell at His feet and told Him, [MARY] "Lord, if You had been here, my brother would not have died!"
[33] [NARRATOR] When Jesus saw her crying, and the Jews who had come with her crying, He was angry in His spirit and deeply moved. [34] [JESUS] "Where have you put him?" [SYMPATHETIC JEWS] "Lord, come and see."
[35] [NARRATOR] Jesus wept.

91

36 [SYMPATHETIC JEWS] "See how He loved him!" 37 [SKEPTICAL JEWS] "Couldn't He who opened the blind man's eyes also have kept this man from dying?"
38 [NARRATOR] Then Jesus, angry in Himself again, came to the tomb. It was a cave, and a stone was lying against it. 39 [JESUS] "Remove the stone."
[MARTHA] "Lord, he already stinks. It's been four days."
40 [JESUS] "Didn't I tell you that if you believed you would see the glory of God?"
41 [NARRATOR] So they removed the stone. Then Jesus raised His eyes and said, [JESUS] "Father, I thank You that You heard Me. 42 I know that You always hear Me, but because of the crowd standing here I said this, so they may believe You sent Me." 43 [NARRATOR] After He said this, He shouted with a loud voice, [JESUS] "Lazarus, come out!" 44 [NARRATOR] The dead man came out bound hand and foot with linen strips and with his face wrapped in a cloth. Jesus said to them, [JESUS] "Loose him and let him go."

Understanding Jesus' Power Over Death

Studies show that clever marketing and ad campaigns do not sell products or fill seats at movies or sporting events—word of mouth does. The millions spent on promoting products are designed to get people talking. Being fully man and fully God, Jesus understood human nature better than anyone. He knew that even in the first-century world, He was going to have to demonstrate His power to conquer death before people would truly grasp His power.

Can you imagine the word of mouth buzz that Jesus generated when He raised Lazarus from the dead? Jesus came into the world to offer each of us life after death: "For God loved the world in this way: He gave His one and only Son, so that everyone who believes in Him will not perish but have eternal life" (John 3:16). Through the resurrection of Lazarus, Jesus demonstrated that He could deliver on that promise. ❸ Jesus demonstrated through miracles that He is a supernatural force that demands the full attention of all mankind, not just another voice in the crowd trying to push His message.

"Lord, if You had been here, my brother wouldn't have died"

As we look at Lazarus' story, there are several key phrases that highlight what the passage is meant to teach us about death, what faith in Jesus can do for us at the time of death, and what happens after death. The first phrase is "Lord, if You had been here, my brother wouldn't have died" (verses 21 and 32). In the context of the story, this is a statement of belief that Jesus could have prevented the death. In the context of our own lives, this phrase voices a feeling many have: "If God had really been here, my friend would not have died." Other statements made from a similar perspective include: I prayed for God to heal my grandmother from cancer, but she still died ... Where was God?!" Or, "I saw on the news that a teenager was abducted and killed – where was God in that situation?" Sometimes we get the idea that

God's primary job is to be our all-powerful, spiritual bodyguard who is supposed to protect us from harm and death. But we are not "bulletproof." In fact, we are all terminal. Physical death happens. Every person in this story, including Lazarus, has long since experienced physical death. While Jesus delayed physical death for Lazarus, He has not eliminated it for any of us. ❹ While all of us will face physical death, our hope is in Jesus because He is God and has ultimate power over death itself. The real death we must be concerned about is the second death— spiritual death.

"I am the resurrection and the life. The one who believes in Me, even though he dies, will live. Everyone who lives and believes in Me will never die—ever."

A second phrase we should look at is in verses 25-26: "I am the resurrection and the life. The one who believes in Me, even though he dies, will live. Everyone who lives and believes in Me will never die—ever." This statement seems to be full of contradictions: "will live, even though he dies" and "everyone who lives and believes in Me will never die—ever." But, Jesus is presenting two different meanings for the word "die." All people die physically, but not all people will die spiritually. Those who trust and hope in Jesus, even though they will die physically one day, will be resurrected in spirit to live forever with God; they will truly never die! That is, in fact, how the Contemporary English Version of the Bible translates verse 26, "Everyone who lives because of faith in me will never really die." This hope is not affected by what happens to the body. Lazarus' body had even started to decay, but Jesus was still able to resurrect him. In this life, our spirits are dependent on our physical selves. If our bodies suffer, our spirits will most often become lethargic and weak. But in the life after this one, through the power of God, our spirits will break free from the weaknesses imposed on our human bodies. In fact, the Apostle Paul tells us that God will replace our physical body with heavenly" or spiritual ones. These bodies will not have the weaknesses and limitations of the physical bodies we have in this life (1 Corinthians 15:35-44). ❺ No one is "bulletproof" in this life. All of our earthly bodies will die physical deaths caused by time, age, and accident. But ... there is hope and continuing spiritual life for those who believe in and follow Jesus!

"Loose him and let him go."

A third key is found in verse 44, "Loose him and let him go." The grave clothes used to prepare Lazarus' body for burial would be binding and limiting for a person who is alive! In a sense, many people in this life are walking around in "grave clothes." Fearing the unknown or death, they become paranoid about every possible danger. For example, every food linked to a disease is avoided. Travel is evaded out of fear that something unpredictable will happen. Some people become so busy avoiding death that they forget to live. That is why Jesus transformed this life by delivering

us from death's grip through the power of the resurrection. Jesus points out in John 10 that Satan is the thief of life, but that He offers a better life than ever dreamed possible. Hebrews 2:14-15 says, "He too shared in their humanity so that by his death he might destroy him who holds the power of death ... and free those who all their lives were held in slavery by their fear of death" (NIV). Throughout Christian history, passionate believers have lived incredible lives of adventurous grace when they understood this concept. The Apostle Paul (tradition tells us he was beheaded in Rome in AD 65) said, ❻ "To live is Christ, and to die gain." (NIV) Pastor Dietrich Bonhoeffer, who was hung in Nazi Germany in 1945 for preaching against the Third Reich, said, "This is the end. For me, the beginning of life." Missionary Jim Elliot, who was murdered by the tribe he was helping, wrote in his journal, ❻ "He is no fool, he who gives that which he cannot keep to gain that which he cannot lose." Ordinary people can achieve extraordinary results for God when they are free from the "grave clothes" of this life. *Jesus has conquered death so that we can be truly free to live a life of no regrets.*

What Jesus did for Lazarus is something much more than a special favor done for a special friend. ❼ It is a demonstration of God's power over death and an illustration of what is to come to everyone who believes in Christ. Invitations to believe are found throughout the story: "The one who believes in me, even if he dies, will live" (verse 25); "Do you believe this?" (verse 26), "Didn't I tell you that if you believed you would see the glory of God?" (verse 40). When we respond and believe, we step out of the "grave clothes" to start a new life that will never end.

 # Do What? *(15 MINUTES)*

Your Legacy

1. Lazarus, Mary, and Martha are often remembered for the roles they played in the resurrection story. Their attitudes and actions helped define their lives. For what type of things and general attitudes do you want to be remembered? If you were to die today, would people remember you for those things or for less positive ones? Why?

2. What do you do to make a positive difference in the lives of people around you? How is the world a better place because of you?

"LOOSE HIM AND LET HIM GO."
❻ "To live is *Christ*, and to die is *gain*."

"He is no fool, he who *gives up* that which he cannot keep to *gain* to that which he cannot lose."

❼ What two things did Jesus' resurrection of Lazarus demonstrate?
1) _____
2) _____

SMALL-GROUP TIME: Ask students to divide back into small groups and discuss the "Do What?" questions. Small-group facilitators should lead the discussions and set the model for openness and honesty in responding.

Be sensitive to and encourage the students' questioning in this area.

3. Will the loved ones you leave behind have any cause to doubt where you will spend eternity? Why or why not?

LifePoint Review

Small-group facilitators should reinforce the LifePoint for this session. Make sure that student's questions are invited and addressed genuinely.

God promises eternal life to those who have a personal relationship with Jesus. That assurance gives Christ-followers hope for the future and drives them to live passionately in the present.

"Do" Points:

These "Do" Points will help you grab hold of this week's LifePoint. This is not a time for typical Sunday School answers as you discuss these questions.

1. <u>Trust Jesus' promise of eternal life.</u> It's one thing to say you trust Christ when life is good. It's another to recognize He is good even in the face of life's greatest tragedies. **Does your life reflect your belief in eternity? Explain.**

2. <u>Learn to talk openly about death.</u> If you know that Jesus has conquered death, then you no longer need to treat death as a fearful subject. You can talk about death in a healthy way with your friends and family because you know it has no lasting power over you. Discussing it will release its grip on you even further. **What could you say to encourage a friend who faces the death of a loved one whose life reflected his or her love for Christ?**

3. <u>Live a "no regrets" life.</u> People who have hope in the eternal life that Jesus provides are wise to remember that each day is a gift from God. **How wisely are you using the time you've been given on earth? What steps can you take to make sure that when you die, you'll have no regrets?**

Prayer Connection:

This is the time to encourage, support, and pray for each other.

Share prayer needs with the group, especially those related to trusting in the hope of eternity through Jesus—even on days when everything seems to be going wrong. Your group facilitator will close your time in prayer.

Prayer Needs:

Encourage students to list prayer needs for others in their books so they can pray for one another during the week. Assign a student coordinator in each small group to gather the group's requests and e-mail them to the group members.

Encourage students to dig a little deeper by completing a "Now What" assignment before the next time you meet. Remind students about the "Get Ready" short daily Bible readings and related questions at the beginning of Session 8.

Make yourself available to anyone with more questions on death and eternal life.

 # now What?

Deepen your understanding of who God is, and continue the journey you've begun today by choosing one of the following assignments to complete this week:

Option #1:
Prayer walk through a cemetery (perhaps visit the grave site of a family member or friend). While there, reflect on your life and the direction you're headed. Ask God to help you make the most of your time on earth.

Option #2:
Write a card or note of encouragement to someone who is struggling with a terminal illness or the ravages of old age. Gently remind them that you are praying for them and that there is hope in Jesus. Use the Scripture verses of this lesson to lift their spirits.

Option #3:
Create a list of things you want to do before you die. Recognizing that Christ has set us free to live passionately (but not foolishly), dream of all the places God might send you in your lifetime and the adventures He might allow you experience. Use the Internet as a research tool and explore Web sites that offer some exciting ministry opportunities available to young people such as the Youth With A Mission (*www.ywam.org*), Teen Mission (*www.teenmissions.org*), International Mission Board (*www.imb.org*), the North American Mission Board (*www.studentz.com*), General Board of Global Missions (*www.gbgm-umc.org*), Campus Crusade for Christ (*www.campuscrusade.com*), Young Life (*www.younglife.org*), and the Billy Graham Evangelistic Association (*www.passageway.org*). Be sure you check the Web pages for your church and denominational missions organizations.

Bible Reference Notes

Use these notes to deepen your understanding as you study the Bible on your own:

John 11:17-44

11:21 if You had been here, my brother wouldn't have died. Since Lazarus had probably died even fore Jesus received the message, and since Martha also adds a statement of trust in Christ's power to do something wonderful "even now" (v. 22), this is not a rebuke but an expression of regret. It implies faith that if Jesus had been on the scene before his death, Lazarus could have survived.

11:22 even now I know. Given her confusion in verse 39, this may not be an expectation that Jesus could do a miracle even now. However, it is an expression of a faith that Christ is in control and will bring about what is best.

11:23 will rise again. The Jewish leaders believed in a general resurrection. She would have understood Jesus' comment as merely an appropriate expression of comfort. Other mourners, wishing to comfort her and assure her they knew Lazarus had been a good man, probably said very similar things to her.

11:25 I am the resurrection and the life. This claim would jar anyone at a funeral! By it, Jesus focuses Martha's attention, not on the doctrine of the general resurrection, but on Him as the source of that resurrection (5:24-29). **even if he dies will live.** Spiritual life will not end at physical death. In this verse and in verse 26, Jesus is asserting His sovereign power over death and His ability to give life "to anyone He wants to" (5:21).

11:26 Do you believe this? Jesus directly confronts Martha with this claim. Does she see Him only as a healer or as the Lord of life? Jesus on several occasions made a point of giving His followers an opportunity to declare where they stood in relationship to Him. A similar instance is when He asked Peter, "But, you? Who do you say that I am?" (Matt. 16:15).

11:27 In this verse, Martha declares in four terms exactly who Jesus is. **Lord.** This can mean simply "sir." Whereas in verse 21 it may have that intent, in this verse the author is using it as a title for Deity since the rest of Martha's statement is full of spiritual insight into His identity. **the Messiah, the Son of God, who was to come into the world.** In calling Him the Christ, Martha acknowledges Jesus as the One who delivers and saves His people from the power of sin and death. The meaning behind this title is that He is God, sharing the Father's essential nature just as a child shares the characteristics of his or her parents. It was this claim to be the Son of God that was the real grounds for the opposition against Him (19:7). The final phrase, "who was to come into the world," refers to the expectation that one day a leader like Moses would arise (Deut.18:18). This too acknowledges His authority and divine commission.

11:32 Mary. That Mary stayed at home when Jesus came (v. 20) seems to indicate despair in the one who had shown so much devotion to Christ in other situations (v. 2; Luke 10:38-42). Also Mary here does not add a statement of faith like Martha expressed, that Jesus could still do something powerful (v. 22). This seems to indicate that when Mary says, "Lord, if You had been here, my brother would not have died," it may have been more an expression of disappointment than faith.

11:33 crying. In contrast to the Western custom of acting restrained at funerals, in this culture they were times for loud, public expressions of grief. The word "crying" here indicates a type of wailing.

11:38 the tomb. Tombs for people of importance were either vertical shafts covered by a stone, or horizontal hollows carved out of a hill. Since this tomb is carved out of a cave, it would be the latter type.

11:39 he already stinks. Even if Martha knew of the others Jesus had raised (Matt. 11:5; Mark 5:22-43; Luke 7:11-15), they were people who had been dead for only a short time. By the fourth day the actual decomposition of the body had begun and therefore no resuscitation could be possible.

11:40 Didn't I tell you. This may be a reference to the message in verse 4, or the implication of what He meant by His declaration to Martha in verse 25. The signs in this Gospel have consistently been regarded as demonstrations of Jesus' identity. They reveal His glory (2:11) and, based on them, people make decisions about who He is (6:14; 9:32-33). This final sign will reveal what has been alluded to all along—Jesus is God.

11:44 bound hand and foot with linen strips. While burial customs included wrapping the body with cloth and spices (19:40), this was not intended to preserve the body, like the ancient Egyptian process of mummification. It only served as a sign of honor for the deceased person.

7

NOTES

Session

8

GET CONNECTED: WHY DO I NEED OTHER CHRISTIANS?

Connections Prep

MAIN LIFEPOINT:

As Christ-followers, we need to connect with others who share our beliefs. As we "do life together" and not just church, we can experience authentic, redemptive community—finding healing, freedom, and growth.

To reinforce the LifePoint, leaders and small-group facilitators should understand the following more detailed CheckPoints and "Do" Points.

BIBLE STUDY CHECKPOINTS:

- · Evaluate the depth of our friendships
- · Understand that God has created us to have relationships with other Christ-followers
- · Acknowledge that every believer needs the church

LIFE CHANGE "DO" POINTS:

- · Commit to "doing life together" with other Christ-followers
- · Seek out a small group in which to experience redemptive community
- · Discover ways to use our gifts and talents to help fulfill the mission Jesus gave the church

PREPARATION:

- ☐ Review the *Leader's Book* for this session and prepare your teaching.
- ☐ Determine how you will subdivide students into small discussion groups.
- ☐ Recruit mature students or adults as small-group facilitators. Be sure these facilitators plan to attend.
- ☐ If possible, set up your meeting room to resemble a coffee house. Put an "Open for Business" sign on the door and serve coffee, hot chocolate, and pastries.

REQUIRED SUPPLIES:

- ☐ *Essential Truth: Inviting Christ into My Reality* Leader books for each group facilitator
- ☐ *Essential Truth: Inviting Christ into My Reality* Student books for each student
- ☐ Pens or pencils for each student
- ☐ A penny for each student

 Get Ready

Read one of these short Bible passages each day and spend a few minutes wrapping your brain around it. Be sure to jot down any insights you discover about living life.

MONDAY

Read 1 Corinthians 12:18-26

Paul compares the different people of the church to the different parts of a human body. What is your least favorite physical feature? What would happen if you did not have that body part? Why is each part important?

TUESDAY

Read Ephesians 5:1-2,18-21

The theme of this section of Ephesians is to "be an imitator of God." Did you ever imitate someone when you were a child? Why? What did you learn about the value of submission when you were little? What value can your determination to submit to God's authorities in your life have for you now?

WEDNESDAY

Read Ephesians 4:1-16

Paul often used the idea of a journey to help explain the Christian life and community. If you were going on a trip, which friends would you invite along? Why would you include some and leave out others?

THURSDAY

Read Matthew 28:18-20

This passage explains our mission as followers of Christ. At first glance, it sounds impossible. But since we know with Christ "all things are possible," what can you do to be a part of this purpose? Can you do it alone? Why or why not?

FRIDAY

Read 1 Peter 5:1-5

Children don't like sharing. Did you have a favorite toy that you hated sharing when friends came over? Now that you are older, do you play well with others? Are you willing to "share" your life with the people around you? Why or why not?

SATURDAY

Read Acts 2:42-47

The early church members literally gave up everything they had and lived together. Could you do that? Spend a few moments imagining funny, awkward, and special moments that might occur if your church family all moved into one house. What draws people together? What keeps them from connecting?

SUNDAY

Read Acts 2:42-47 again

The Bible repeatedly teaches us to do what God says, and assures us He will take care of the results. How did God respond to the commitment level of these early Christians? Do people in your community see a real difference in the lives of those in your church? Why or why not?

8

LARGE-GROUP OPENING:
Get everyone's attention. Make announcements. Open your session with a prayer. Read the LifePoint to the students.

 LifePoint

As Christ-followers, we need to connect with others who share our beliefs. As we "do life together" and not just church, we can experience authentic, redemptive community—finding healing, freedom, and growth.

SMALL-GROUP TIME:
Instruct students to separate into smaller groups of 4-8, preferably in a circle configuration. Call on the mature student or adult leaders you recruited to facilitate each small group through this "Say What?" segment.

Say What? *(15 MINUTES)*

Random Question of the Week:

The ancient Romans bathed often, yet a few hundred years later—during The Renaissance—people in the same general region seldom or never washed themselves. Why did people suddenly avoid cleanliness?

Group Experience: Penny Universities

· A penny for each student

Say something like, "We all know that companies like Starbucks® and Seattle's Best™ have made the local coffee shop *the* place to hang out today. But did you know that the coffeehouse is not a new invention at all? In the 1700's there were over 2,000 coffeehouses in the city of London alone. Since scholars, tradesmen, politicians, and poets frequented them, they became known as "penny universities." For many who lacked resources to attend the exclusive university system, those interested in ideas could come in, buy coffee or tea for a penny, and engage in conversation that would teach them more about many topics than a traditional university class. Since it took some time to enjoy a hot beverage, and Styrofoam™ had yet to be invented for portability, these meetinghouses soon became key places in communities for people to connect and for ideas and influences to spread."

"Most of you have the heard the phrase, "a penny for your thoughts." This saying originated in penny universities. I'm going to give you each a penny. When I hand it to you, tell us in two or three sentences exactly why you are participating in this Life Connections group study. Briefly explain what's in it for you."

After everyone has had a chance to respond, ask the following:

1. It's Friday night, and you have nothing to do. Which of these options would you choose to fill your time?
   - ☐ Chill by myself and catch up on sleep
   - ☐ Do my homework
   - ☐ Hang out with my folks
   - ☐ Go out with that cute guy or girl I've been obsessing over
   - ☐ Meet with friends for pizza and a round of mini-golf
   - ☐ Call my best friend and brainstorm something exciting to do
   - ☐ Other: _____

2. Why do you think interaction with others is an important part of your spiritual journey?

3. What similarities should a local church or student ministry share with penny universities?

LARGE-GROUP TIME:
Have the students turn to face the front for this teaching time. Be sure you can make eye contact with each student in the room. Encourage students to follow along and take notes in their *Student Books.*

Share the "So What?" information with your large group of students. You may modify it with your own perspectives and teaching needs. Be sure to highlight the underlined information, which gives answers to the *Student Book* questions and fill-in-the-blanks (shown in your margins).

 # So What? *(30 MINUTES)*

Teaching Outline

I. Relationship: The Foundation of the Church
A. Humans are addicted to relationships
B. Relationships allow people to feel that they matter
C. Be intentional about offering the world something it can't live without
D. Early church: body committed to learning, growing, & serving

II. Acts 2:42-47

III. Created for Connection – "Can You Hear Me Now?"
A. We are "wired" & "connected" (3 billion Internet, 40 billion e-mails daily)
B. If we are so connected with technology, why do we feel so disconnected?
C. One meaningful conversation this week? One real friend? Lonely & hurting?
D. God made us to enjoy relationships, and He gave us a community
E. Even though our world is becoming more disconnected, God created us for connecting with Him & others
F. How are we doing?

IV. Impossible to do on our own
A. Acts 2:44 intriguing: "*All* the believers were together and *had everything in common.*"
B. We must recognize that we need each other
   1. Church is God's plan to bring healing & freedom to His people
   2. Through us God will complete His mission of setting captives free and healing the broken-hearted (see Isaiah 61:1-2)

V. Awesome results of "doing life together" in church

A. People's physical & spiritual needs are met

B. Holy Spirit, working through the church, does the impossible

C. Love, sincerity, & thanksgiving are the way of daily life

D. Other people notice what God is doing & are drawn in

E. NOTE: even the early church started having problems

F. We need to get connected with other Christ-followers to grow relationally, spiritually, & missionally

TEACHING FOR THE LARGE GROUP:

❶ Humans are addicted to *relationships*.

❷ Relationships allow people to feel that they *matter*.

❸ What should the church be intentional about offering the world?

❹ Luke described the early church as God intended it: a *body* of believers committed to *learning*, *growing*, and *serving*.

Learning from the Bible ...

Acts 2:42-47

Ask a volunteer to come to the front of the room and read it.

Relationship: The Foundation of the Church

❶ Humans are addicted to relationships. They are the subjects of talk shows, the heart behind uplifting slogans on t-shirts and greeting cards, and they are the reasons that holidays such as Christmas and Valentine's Day prove so valuable to producers. For a time, our fast-paced culture focused more on the individual than on the couple, the family, or the group. This tendency, however, has changed. Marketing now reflects a simple truth: ❷ relationships allow people to feel that they matter. And if a company can tap into a person's relational need, that company will likely find success in building support for their product.

The church has been telling the world that relationships matter for more than 2,000 years. But recently, publicized instances of power trips, church politics, and poor application of biblical truth have unfairly portrayed the church as one of the least caring and most judgmental segments of society. If the church is going to recapture the hearts of a generation, we must lead in the movement to build nurturing, meaningful relationships. ❸ Churches should be intentional about offering the world something it can't live without: lives lived in community that are built on truth and lead to a greater sense of purpose. In this type of community, members realize they are part of something greater than themselves. They find value and a sense that what they do matters on a community scale. ❹ Luke captures this beautifully in Acts 2. He describes the early church learning, growing, and serving as one body as God intended.

Learning from the Bible

⁴² *And they devoted themselves to the apostles' teaching, to fellowship, to the breaking of bread, and to prayers.*
⁴³ *Then fear came over everyone, and many wonders and signs were being performed through the apostles.* ⁴⁴ *Now all the believers were together and had everything in common.* ⁴⁵ *So they sold their possessions and property and distributed the proceeds to all,*

as anyone had a need. 46 And every day they devoted themselves [to meeting] together in the temple complex, and broke bread from house to house. They ate their food with gladness and simplicity of heart, 47 praising God and having favor with all the people. And every day the Lord added to them those who were being saved.

Created for Connection – "Can You Hear Me Now?"

We are "wired" and "connected" in ways our grandparents could never have imagined 50 or 60 years ago. It is estimated that three billion people have regular access to the Internet, and that number is growing. Daily, 40 billion e-mails are sent by businesspeople, family, and friends trying to catch up and stay connected. But this easy access approach to communication leads to an important question: if we are so connected through technology, why do we feel so disconnected from others? If we can instantly send a message to the other side of the world, why do we rarely talk with the neighbor who lives across the street? If we can cross continents on the Web before our parents allow us to cross the street by ourselves, why are we so reluctant to cross to the other side of the lunchroom to make a new friend?

Think about your answers to the following questions. Have you had at least one meaningful conversation with someone this week? Can you name at least one friend who would do anything for you? Are you lonely and hurting? It's tough to feel like you matter in this impersonal world. ❺ Today you'll be reminded that God made us to enjoy relationships, and He gave us a community—the church—in which we can spiritually grow and live out His purposes for our lives alongside other Christ-followers.

In the midst of our struggles, we should remember that ❻ even though our world is becoming more disconnected, God created us for connecting with Him and others. There are many ways that we see God's design for relationship. One reality is that God Himself exists in relationship within the Trinity—God the Father, God the Son, and God the Holy Spirit. While it hurts our heads to figure out how all three are God and God is One at the same time, we can't deny the reality that relationship is a theme woven throughout life. The Bible also teaches that we were created for intimate relationships of trust. Soon after the creation of man, God Himself noted in Genesis 2:18 that "it is not good for the man to be alone." Genesis 2:24 instructs: "a man leaves his father and mother and bonds with his wife." This verse points to complete intimacy in loyalty, trust, commitment, and affection. It mirrors what our relationship with God should look like. This theme was a key value of the first churches. Luke describes the church in Acts as a people who "devoted themselves"

LARGE-GROUP TIME CONTINUED:
This is the meat of the teaching time. Remind students to follow along and take notes in their *Student Books*.

As you share the "So What?" information with students, make it your own.

Emphasize underlined information, which gives key points, answers to the *Student Book* questions or fill-in-the-blanks in the (shown in your margins).

❺ Why did God give us the church community?

❻ For what purposes did God create us?

8

to growing together and put aside differences as "all the believers were together and had everything in common." How do your friendships compare to this description of community? Is your loneliness a result of your attempt to "do life" on your own, or have you honestly tried to drop your guard and let others into your life? Remember, if we're going to grow spiritually, we must honestly evaluate the condition of our current relationships and decide to pursue true, honest, redemptive community with those on the journey with us.

This is almost impossible to do on our own. Even the most committed people around us are likely to give up after awhile. Verse 44 is the intriguing passage for most of us. It states, "*All* the believers were together and *had everything in common.*" How is that even possible? All of us have had frustrating experiences when we even try to get a group of five or six to pick a restaurant or a movie, let alone to be in agreement about *everything*. Here it is important to note the big picture. The Holy Spirit was moving in a fresh, new way in their world and in their lives. The first Christians went from walking with Jesus, to seeing Him murdered, to being overjoyed at His resurrection all in a very short time. They had been scattered, confused, and hurt, but the resurrection of Jesus and the power of the Holy Spirit combined with the power of purpose and meaning to form them into a potent missionary force that changed the world. They "devoted themselves" to learning from leaders who had been with Jesus, nurturing their relationships with other Christ-followers, and serving others in the name of Jesus, and they gained a perspective of unity that they had never experienced before. Christian unity does not negate the idea that we are different people with different personalities and unique qualities. Instead, it shapes those differences into a common purpose that is more important than any personal quirks we might have. In other words, the first church grasped that they were part of something much bigger than themselves. Likewise, ❼ we must recognize that we need each other because the church is God's plan to bring healing and freedom to His people, and through us to complete His mission of setting captives free and healing the broken-hearted (see Isaiah 61:1-2).

The results of "doing life together" in church as God intended are awesome. People's physical and spiritual needs are met. The Holy Spirit, working through the church, does things that people previously thought impossible, changing lives and restoring hope. Love, sincerity, and thanksgiving are no longer vague ideas but the way of daily life. ❽ Other people can't help but notice what God is doing, and they are drawn into these communities by love and acceptance.

We have to confess that our churches today often fall far, far short of this awesome picture of what God had in mind. Even the early church started having problems as we see just a few chapters later. Some felt neglected (e.g. Acts 6:1-7), some fought

❼ The *church* is God's plan designed to bring His people together around the cause of Christ for the mission of *changing the world*.

We need each other because *the church* is God's plan to bring *healing* and *freedom* to His people, and through us to complete His *mission* of setting captives free and healing the broken-hearted (see Isaiah 61:1-2).

❽ Other people can't help but notice what God is doing, and they are drawn into these communities by *love* and *acceptance*.

over church leadership (e.g. 1 Corinthians 1:10-17), and some disagreed over cultural issues (Galatians 2:11-14). I'm sure each of us can easily list issues we have with the church in general and our church in particular. But that doesn't mean we should write off the church as irrelevant. We can't keep "dating the church" by trying out new groups forever until we find one that is "perfect." We have to prayerfully and intentionally find a place where we can love, grow, and serve. People have tried for centuries to figure it out some other way, but the truth remains the same: ❾ <u>We need to get connected with other Christ-followers in order to grow relationally, spiritually, and missionally</u>. Let's be part of the solution, not part of the problem!

❾ Why we need to get connected with other followers of Christ?

SMALL-GROUP TIME:
Use this time to help students begin to integrate the truth they've learned into their lives while they connect with the other students in the group, the leaders, and with God.

Ask students to divide back into small groups and discuss the "Do What?" questions. Small-group facilitators should lead the discussions and set the model by connecting with the students.

 # Do What? *(15 MINUTES)*

Understanding Community

1. What is it about a close group of friends that makes you feel welcome and safe—with whom you can share anything?

If you had lived during the time of the early church described in the Acts passage, which of its qualities would you have found most appealing?

□ Devotion to the apostles' teaching

□ Signs and wonders (miracles) that were done in their midst

□ The way they cared and sacrificed for each other

□ The way they shared their meals and lives together

□ The way they impacted the world with the good news of Jesus

8

3. How well does your church measure up against the close community described in Luke's account? Explain.

4. Which of the following do you most need your church to provide right now?

□ Teaching from the Bible

□ A sense of belonging

□ Worship that draws me closer to God

□ A safe place to talk about my concerns

□ Advice on how to live

□ Other: _____

LifePoint Review

As Christ-followers, we need to connect with others who share our beliefs. As we "do life together" and not just church, we can experience authentic, redemptive community—finding healing, freedom, and growth.

"Do" Points:

These "Do" Points will help you grab hold of this week's LifePoint. Make an effort to connect with each other as you discuss the questions within your small group.

1. Commit to "doing life together" with other Christ-followers. If you weren't made to go to church, would you go? Statistics show that only about 2 out of 10 students who are active in church throughout high school take the initiative to get connected to a church during their college years.
What plans will you make to be sure you get involved in a local church when you leave home? Why is it important that you do? What kind of things will you look for in a church?

2. Seek out a small group in which to experience redemptive community. For much of the first century, churches were small and most met secretly in homes or even underground. It's important to remember that we do not go to church; we are the church. We all need to be in an intimate relationship with others who share our faith. In a group like this we can be fully known, loved, and cared for.
Are you a regular member of a small group of church friends? If so, how do you benefit from your relationship with them? If not, explain.

3. Find ways to use your gifts and talents to accomplish the mission of the church. Many people "shop" for churches based on their preferences and likes, instead of prayerfully considering which local group God is calling them to be a part of. While every Christ-follower needs to be part of a Christ-focused church that helps them to celebrate and grow spiritually, we also need to consider how our gifts and talents can be used to serve that church.
What are your spiritual gifts? Have you thought about how you can use your talents to help grow the church and share the story of Jesus? Who can help you find ways to get connected and give of your life to the church?

Prayer Connection:

This is the time to encourage, support, and pray for each other in our journeys to grasp the importance of relationships to our spiritual growth.

Share prayer needs with the group, especially those related to finding and connecting with other Christ-followers who will help you to feel loved and accepted while learning more about God's plan for you. Your group facilitator will close your time in prayer.

Prayer Needs:

now What?

8

Deepen your understanding of who God is, and continue the journey you've begun today by, choosing one of the following assignments to complete this week:

Option #1:
List friends who need to "connect" to the church. Pray for each of them by name, and reflect on ways you can help them get plugged in. Write down one way you'll encourage each of them to find the relationships or church home they need. If you are struggling with church life, prayerfully list the issues you are wrestling with. Then commit to setting up a time to share your issues with a parent, trusted adult leader, or student minister.

Option #2:
Take a prayer walk around your church. Bring a friend with you if possible, and be sure to tell someone on staff or the church receptionist what you are doing. As you walk around the building, pray for each ministry your church has as well as the leader who serves in that area. Pray that God will use your church as a "base" from which the surrounding community and the world can be reached. Ask God to reveal how you can use your gifts to serve through your church's ministries.

Option #3:

Write a card or note of encouragement to your senior pastor or student minister. Share with them that you are praying for them and that you are ready to serve and help your church become what God intends for it to be.

Bible Reference notes

Use these notes to deepen your understanding as you study the Bible on your own:

Acts 2:42-47

2:42 devoted themselves. The four components of the church's life here may represent what occurred at their gatherings. *teaching.* The foundation for the church's life was the instruction given by the apostles as the representatives of Jesus. *fellowship.* Literally, "sharing." While this may include the aspect of sharing to meet material needs (v. 45), it most likely refers to their common participation in the Spirit as they worshipped together (1 Cor. 12). *the breaking of bread.* The Lord's Supper in which they remembered His death (Luke 22:19) and recognized His presence among them (Luke 24:30-31). *prayers.* This may refer to set times and forms of prayer—the typical practice of the Jews.

2:43-47 The picture of the church is one of continual growth (v. 47) marked by generous sharing (vv. 44-45) and joyful worship and fellowship (vv. 46-47). The worship at the temple continued as before since the line dividing Christianity from Judaism had not yet been drawn. Christians simply saw their faith as the natural end of what the Jewish faith had always declared.

2:44-45 everything in common. The shared life that these early Christians practiced was simply an outgrowth of the intense love people had for each other through Jesus Christ. They believed that in Christ each person's need should in some sense become everyone's need. This attitude is a key component to authentic Christian community today as well.

2:47 every day the Lord added to them. Growth in the church was a natural result of the love, fellowship, and commitment to the apostle's teaching that these early Christians lived out.

Matthew 28:18-20

28:18-20 Jesus came near and said to them. This is what has been called the "Great Commission." Because all authority in heaven and earth now belongs to Jesus, He sends His disciples to spread His message everywhere with the promise that He Himself is with them to the end of time.

28:18 All authority has been given to Me in heaven and on earth. This is the meaning of the statement "Jesus is Lord." Since there is no power greater than His (Rom. 8:38-39; Phil. 2:9-11; Col. 1:15-20), there is no other loyalty to which His disciples can give their absolute allegiance.

28:19 Go, therefore. In light of Jesus' authority, He sends His people on a mission. *and make disciples.* Literally, this is "as you are going, make disciples." *of all nations.* There are no geographic, racial, ethnic, or national realms that are outside of the authority and concern of Jesus. *baptizing them.* Baptism was a sign of discipleship and faith. *in the name of the Father and of the Son and of the Holy Spirit.* This is a clear Trinitarian formula. While the doctrine of the Trinity was not clearly articulated and documented until the third century, the roots of its teaching are clearly seen here. There is one name (or character) that defines the triune God.

28:20 teaching them to observe everything I have commanded you. The stress here is on the ethical dimensions of Christian living. Discipleship is practicing the way of life advocated and exemplified by one's master. *I am with you always.* This is the climactic promise of the New Covenant. The presence of God with His people was always the goal toward which Israel looked under the Old Covenant. In Jesus, that presence is assured through the indwelling of Christ's Spirit (John 14:16-17). *to the end of the age.* This covers all time until the return of Christ when the new heaven and the new earth will be revealed.

Session

9

VINTAGE FAITH: HOW DO I KEEP IT REAL?

Connections Prep

MAIN LIFEPOINT: Following Jesus is not about painting on a fake smile and being religious. God wants genuine relationships with us that are characterized by authenticity and integrity.

To reinforce the LifePoint, leaders and small-group facilitators should understand the following more detailed CheckPoints and "Do" Points.

BIBLE STUDY CHECKPOINTS:
- Understand that "religion" is full of people who miss the point and get hung up on rules
- Examine how Jesus reacted to religious people who were full of themselves but not full of God
- Weigh the honesty and integrity of our own hearts

LIFE CHANGE "DO" POINTS:
- Commit to modeling an authentic life that represents the way Jesus lived
- Confront the temptation to put on a false front with other Christ-followers
- Focus on what pleases God, not other people

PREPARATION:
- ☐ Review the *Leader's Book* for this session and prepare your teaching.
- ☐ Determine how you will subdivide students into small discussion groups.
- ☐ Recruit mature students or adults as small-group facilitators. Be sure these facilitators plan to attend.

REQUIRED SUPPLIES:
- ☐ *Essential Truth: Inviting Christ into My Reality* Leader books for each group facilitator
- ☐ *Essential Truth: Inviting Christ into My Reality* Student books for each student
- ☐ Pens or pencils for each student
- ☐ Real $1 bill for each small group
- ☐ Play money $1 bill for each small group
- ☐ Markers and a tear sheet (or poster) for each small group

 Get Ready

Focus on one short Bible passages each day, and spend a few minutes examine your own beliefs. Be sure to capture your discoveries on these journal pages.

MONDAY **Read Luke 11:37**
The religious leaders called "Pharisees" constantly gave Jesus a hard time, yet He chose to eat with them. Would you eat with someone who picks on you? Why do you think Jesus set this model for us?

TUESDAY **Read Luke 11:38-41**
Jesus often made points with His actions, instead of just His words. What was Jesus trying to teach these guys? Have anyone's actions recently caught you off guard? What did that person's behavior tell you about his or her character?

WEDNESDAY **Read Luke 11:42-44**
The Pharisees were supposed to be experts on the subject of God. But while they could follow rigid rules meant to please Him, they always seemed to miss out when it came to understanding God's heart and intent. Have you ever acted like a Pharisee, working hard to please God without grasping His love and plan for you?

THURSDAY **Read Luke 11:45-46**
Nobody likes to be overwhelmed. When was the last time you felt totally swamped? Who or what made you feel that way? How did you cope?

FRIDAY

Read Luke 11:47-51

Every generation has its defining moments. What memorable events in history have most shaped you and your friends? For what will your generation be remembered?

SATURDAY

Read Luke 11:52

This verse gives a strong warning to leaders who don't help people get closer to God. What could leaders in the church today do to help people focus on God? What mistakes do leaders sometimes make as they try to grow churches or organizations?

SUNDAY

Read Luke 11:53-54

An old saying goes, "What is right is not always popular, and what is popular is not always right." Have you ever gotten into trouble for telling the truth? How does it feel to stand up for what you believe in?

9

LARGE-GROUP OPENING:
Get everyone's attention. Make announcements. Open your session with a prayer. Read the LifePoint to the students.

 LifePoint

Following Jesus is not about painting on a fake smile and being religious. God wants genuine relationships with us that are characterized by authenticity and integrity.

SMALL-GROUP TIME:
Instruct students to
separate into smaller
groups of 4-8, prefer-
ably in a circle con-
figuration. Call on the
mature student or adult
leaders you recruited
to facilitate each small
group through this "Say
What?" segment.

 # Say What? *(15 MINUTES)*

Random Question of the Week:
Why do people have uvulas—those little hangy, fleshy lobes in the back of
the mouth?

Group Experience: The Real Thing

- A real $1 bill
- Play money $1 bill
- Markers and a tear sheet or poster

Tell the students they are part of a counterfeit investigation team. Explain that the
treasury has been swamped with fake dollar bills. They will be given a real bill to
study in order to create a list of counterfeit detection points that can be shared
with local banks and businesses.

Give the students a real dollar bill. Tell them to study it carefully, making a list of
the bill's specific details on their poster or tear sheet.

After a few minutes, say something like, "Instead of training their experts in all the
different ways to counterfeit money, the Treasury Department immerses their team
in the real thing. Experts examine and study real currency until they memorize the
markings that make each denomination distinct. The anti-counterfeiting experts
become so familiar with the original, they can spot a fake almost instantly."

Give the students the play $1 bill. Ask them to quickly brainstorm three things
about it that identify it as a fake. (Don't worry if the play money looks nothing like
the real thing. It's OK to let students state the obvious.)

After the activity, ask the following:

1. As you made your list of counterfeit detection points, you noticed many government seals and symbols designed to set the dollar bill apart as legitimately
belonging to the U.S. treasury. What specific signs or indicators do you expect to
see in someone who is a true follower of Christ?

2. Christian author Brennan Manning said, "The single greatest cause of atheism
in the world today is Christians who proclaim Jesus with their lips and then deny

him with their lifestyles. It is what an unbelieving world finds simply unbeliev-able." Manning referred to counterfeit Christ-followers: those who claim to be Christians but live no differently than those who don't have any connection to Jesus. What behaviors and attitudes might lead people to question a Christ-follower's sincerity?

3. Who should we pattern our lives after: other Christians or Jesus? Why is this dis-tinction important?

  # So What? *(30 MINUTES)*

Teaching Outline

I. State of the Church
   A. Only 26% of Americans attend church (marked decrease in each generation)
   B. Why continued dramatic decrease in church participation?
   C. Jesus consistently valued people over programs and traditions

II. Luke 11:37-54

III. Famous Last Words – Western Union 1880s
   A. So focused on improving telegraph, they ignored much greater innovation
   B. Unfortunately, too many who claim to follow God get so hung up too

9

IV. God Doesn't Want Religious Puppets!
   A. God promised if you obey My commands I'll have relationship with you
   B. Israelites not faithful & soon forgot whole point of relationship
   C. When Jesus came things were turned inside out
   D. God desires a genuine relationship with us lived out with authenticity
   E. Jesus' radical claim in John 8:31-32: "Truth" is a person—Jesus Christ

V. Confusing Religion & Relationship
   A. Easier to live by a set of rules than by a relationship
   B. A relationship takes constant nurturing & it's changing

C. Authentic faith not supposed to be safe!

D. Life is an adventure in God's grace as He changes our lives & hearts

E. Bible's rules keep us safely under protection of God who loves us

VI. Jesus' Challenge

A. Live from inside out; clean up hearts, not just outward appearances

B. How would we measure up if Jesus came today to hang out with us?

C. Focus on relationship vs. religion

**TEACHING FOR THE
LARGE GROUP**

❶ What "serious
problem" faces
the church?

❷ How, according
to some research, is
the church perceived
by the younger
generation?
☐ As a social club
for the religious
☐ As a loving place
of acceptance
and forgiveness
☐ As a university
designed to teach
religious knowledge
☐ As a great place
to find a date for
Friday night

❸ The church is
sometimes seen as a
place full of *judgment*
and *self-absorption*.
But what was it
intended to do?

❹ Jesus consistently
valued *people*
over *programs*
and *traditions*.

❺ Jesus searched not
for rigid adherence to
the law, but for ...
☐ Goodness
☐ Commitment
to the law
☐ Authentic faith

The State of the Church

The secret's out. We are no longer a Christian nation. Over the past 30 years, only 40 to 43% of Americans have claimed to attend church each week. However, studies show that Americans have been inflating those numbers. New research suggests that only 26% of Americans actually attend church, and that is the good news. A marked decrease in church attendance is found as one follows the generational chain. While 52% of those born before 1946 attend services, only 36% of the generation born before 1986 attend.[1] Numbers are not yet solid on the generation following these, but the church in America is clearly faced with a serious problem.

Why ❶ the continued dramatic decrease in church participation? ❷ Some research suggests that many young people view church a "social club" for the religious. They hear, "If you follow my rules, dress like I dress, like the music I like, and vote the way I vote, you are accepted." As a result of this general misunderstanding, the church has become less about a relationship between God and people and has become more like an institution of rigid rules, structures, and a "What's in it for me?" mentality. In other words, ❸ church is seen as a place of judgment and self-absorption that has little to do with sharing God's love as it was intended to do.

Jesus was never shy about confronting empty religion that lacked a true relationship with the living God, and the Book of Revelation reveals that He was especially critical of churches who focused on anything but loving God and pointing others to Him. ❹ He consistently valued people over programs and traditions, and won over the hearts and minds of people everywhere He went. Jesus chose to mix with everyone, and He challenged people's way of thinking – whether they were members of the established religious ruling class, poor fishermen, or His closest friends. Everywhere He went, ❺ Jesus searched not for religious adherence to the law but for authentic faith: true belief in God that is characterized by the desire to have relationship with Him.

Learning from
the Bible ...

Luke 11:37-54

Ask for three volun-
teers to come to the
front and read the parts
of (1) the narrator,
(2) Jesus, and (3) the
expert in the law.

Learning from the Bible

[NARRATOR] [37] *As [Jesus] was speaking, a Pharisee asked Him to dine with him. So He went in and reclined at the table.* [38] *When the Pharisee saw this, he was amazed that He did not first perform the ritual washing.* [39] *But the Lord said to him: [JESUS] "Now you Pharisees clean the outside of the cup and dish, but inside you are full of greed and evil.* [40] *Fools! Didn't He who made the outside make the inside too?* [41] *But give to charity what is within, and then everything is clean for you.*

[42] *"But woe to you Pharisees! You give a tenth of mint, rue, and every kind of herb, and you bypass justice and love for God. These things you should have done without neglect-ing the others.* [43] *"Woe to you Pharisees! You love the front seat in the synagogues and greetings in the marketplaces.* [44] *"Woe to you! You are like unmarked graves; the people who walk over them don't know it."*

[45] *[NARRATOR] One of the experts in the law answered Him, [EXPERT IN THE LAW] "Teacher, when You say these things You insult us too."*

[46] *[JESUS] "Woe also to you experts in the law! You load people with burdens that are hard to carry, yet you yourselves don't touch these burdens with one of your fingers.* [47] *"Woe to you! You build monuments to the prophets, and your fathers killed them.* [48] *Therefore you are witnesses that you approve the deeds of your fathers, for they killed them, and you build their monuments.* [49] *Because of this, the wisdom of God said, 'I will send them prophets and apostles, and some of them they will kill and persecute,'* [50] *so that this generation may be held responsible for the blood of all the prophets shed since the foundation of the world,* — [51] *from the blood of Abel to the blood of Zechariah, who perished between the altar and the sanctuary.*

"Yes, I tell you, this generation will be held responsible.

[52] *"Woe to you experts in the law! You have taken away the key of knowledge! You didn't go in yourselves, and you hindered those who were going in."*

[NARRATOR] [53] *When He left there, the scribes and the Pharisees began to oppose Him fiercely and to cross-examine Him about many things;* [54] *they were lying in wait for Him to trap Him in something He said.*

God Doesn't Want Religious Puppets!

Famous Last Words

LARGE-GROUP TIME
CONTINUED:
This is the meat of the
teaching time. Remind
students to follow along
and take notes in their
Student Books.

In the 1880's, Western Union—the company that pioneered the use of the telegraph for long-distance communication—was so focused on improving the telegraph's speed and technology that they ignored a much greater innovation in communica-tion. In their focus to perfect the telegraph that would soon become obsolete, they made this internal memo about a silly gadget invented by Alexander Graham Bell: "This 'telephone' has too many shortcomings to be seriously considered as a means of communication. The device is inherently of no value to us."

9

117

---

❻ When Jesus came to earth, He taught that man's connection to God is not about following a *religious* way of life. God desires a genuine *relationship* with us.

❼ "Religion" is done, not to build a relationship with God, but to ...
☐ Impress God and win Brownie points
☐ Appease God and show off personal goodness and spirituality
☐ Gain the respect of angels and to avoid hell

Unfortunately, too many people who claim to follow God get so hung up on only following the Ten Commandments, busily contributing to community programs, and insisting that the church conduct the weekly worship service in just such-and-such a way that they never develop true relationships with God. Like Western Union, they get so focused on the process of perfecting their own product—works designed to impress God—that they altogether write off the incredibly life-changing gift of personal relationship that He offers.

God Doesn't Want Religious Puppets!

In the Old Testament, God made a promise to the nation of Israel: If they would obey His commands and decrees, He would a have relationship with them. But the Israelites weren't very faithful to following the rules, and they soon forgot that the whole point of following them was to maintain relationship with God. So by the time God broke into history in the person of Jesus, the Jewish way of life was all about following a complicated set of rules in an attempt not to honor a friendship with God, but to earn His favor. The idea of a relationship with Him had been lost, and Judaism had degenerated into a socio-political system that ensured the power of a few wealthy, educated Jews. It had nothing to do with pointing a lost and hurting world toward a true and loving God.

❻ When Jesus came to earth, He taught that man's connection to God is not about following a religious way of life. God doesn't want to make us religious, obedient puppets! He desires a genuine relationship with us that's lived out with authenticity and integrity. **❼** "Religion," or church done to appease God or to "show off" goodness or spirituality is done by people who miss the point and get hung up on rules. Jesus made a radical claim to the Jews who followed His teachings in John 8: "If you continue in my word, you really are My disciples. You will know the truth, and the truth will set you free" (John 8: 31-32). It is clear that this "truth" is not some vague concept floating around somewhere that we can obtain by following a set of rules. Rather, "truth" is a person. His name is Jesus Christ, and we come to know Him through a relationship with Him!

Confusing Religion and Relationship

So, why do "religious" people confuse religion and relationship with God so easily? First, it's easier to live by a set of rules than by a relationship. A set of rules can be crossed off, completed, and set aside. A relationship, on the other hand, takes constant nurturing. You have to share and give in relationship. You have to learn, grow, and change as well. Second, there is safety in knowing exactly what the rules are. If they are stated clearly, people don't have to think for themselves; they simply have to follow the rules. But vintage (or authentic) faith is not supposed to be safe! It is supposed to be an adventure in God's grace as He changes our lives and hearts.

8 What are the rules given in the Bible meant to do?

After all, **8** the rules He gives us in the Bible are not meant to make us impressive God-robots and obeying them won't earn us Brownie points with God. Instead, they are given as helpful boundaries that keep us safely under the protection of God who loves us.

9 Jesus wanted the religious leaders of His day to clean up their *hearts*.

It's interesting to note how **9** Jesus challenged the religious leaders of His day to live from the inside out; He wanted them to clean up their hearts, not just their outward appearances. It is easy to point fingers and criticize the Pharisees for missing the point. But as a young child once pointed out, "If you point at someone else, three fingers of your own are pointing back at you!" If we are going to be authentic followers of Christ, we must search our hearts. We must ask, "How would we measure up if Jesus physically came back to earth today to hang out with us in our student ministry and in our church? Would He find us self-absorbed with our own new code of religiosity, or would He find us loving God and people in our schools, communities, and churches?"

10 What can Christ-followers do to keep their relationships with God "real"?

We must not get pulled into a lifestyle that's more about religion than relationship. We have to submit ourselves to what God's Word says. Instead of coming to the Bible with an attitude of arrogance or looking at it like a giant rule book, we need to place ourselves under its teaching, allowing the Holy Spirit to challenge and convict us when we get it wrong and to encourage us in our pursuit to know more about God who loves us. **10** Every Christ-follower should strive to "keep it real." Staying connected to God and other Christ-followers is the best way to make sure that happens!

SMALL-GROUP TIME: Use this time to help students begin to integrate the truth they've learned into their lives . Small-group facilitators should lead the discussions and set the model for being open and honest in responding to questions

 # Do What? *(15 MINUTES)*

Out to Impress?

1. In Luke 11:39, Jesus talked about the inside of "the cup and dish" being dirty, while the outside was clean. What attitudes, thoughts, or biases do you hold inside that make you feel less than clean? How can you feel clean?

2. The religious leaders of Jesus' time were hung up on impressing people. They were more concerned with other people's opinion of them than about God's opinion. What "religious" things do you see people do in their efforts to appease God and win the approval of others? Do you think anyone is impressed by their efforts? Are you?

3. If you could start your walk with Jesus all over again, what would you do differently? What will you do differently now?

 # LifePoint Review

Following Jesus is not about painting on a fake smile and being religious. God wants genuine relationships with us that are characterized by authenticity and integrity.

"Do" Points:

These "Do" Points will help you grab hold of this week's LifePoint. Be open and honest as you answer the questions within your small group.

1. Commit to modeling an authentic life that represents the way Jesus lived. We can't control what everyone else thinks about the Christian faith. But we can control the way we live, what we share, and our lifestyle. We can fight charges of hypocrisy by modeling our lives after Jesus. **What can you do to make sure you life models Christ? Consider the temptations you face. What would Jesus definitely not do?**

2. Confess the temptation to put on a false front in front of other Christ-followers. We shouldn't just "try" to be authentic followers of Jesus. We should train ourselves to be open and honest with a committed group of believing friends about our struggles. **What issues are you dealing with that the support of Christian friends might help you overcome? Why is admitting your weaknesses difficult?**

3. Focus on pleasing God, not other people. If we try to spend our lives pleasing everyone, we will end up exhausted and frustrated in emotional prisons of our own making! But a healthy respect of what God thinks about our lives will give us the freedom to live authentically and with integrity.
Have you ever wanted to please people so badly that you stopped being concerned about what God thought about you? If so, tell the group about it.

Be sure to end your session by asking students to share prayer needs with one another, especially as they relate to issues brought up by today's session.

Encourage students to list prayer needs for others in their books so they can pray for one another during the week. Assign a student coordinator in each small group to gather the group's requests and e-mail them to the group members.

Prayer Connection:

This is the time to encourage, support, and pray for each other in our journeys to grasp that God doesn't want us to be religious puppets. He desires genuine relationships with us. He wants us to "be real" in our commitment to Him.

Share prayer needs with the group, especially those related to living your life to please and honor God instead of others or yourself. Your group facilitator will close you time in prayer.

Prayer Needs:

Encourage students to dig a little deeper by completing a "Now What?" assignment before the next time you meet. Remind students about the "Are You Ready?" short daily Bible readings and related questions at the beginning of Session 10. Remind them too they are loved and have a group of people here who want to connect with them!

 **now What?**

Deepen your understanding of who God is, and continue the journey you've begun today by choosing one of the following assignments to complete this week:

Option #1:
Taking your cue from a Benedictine Monk who wrote *Practicing the Presence of God*, shock your parents by offering to do the dishes sometime this week. Use the act of service as a time of worship and praise. As you work, reflect on Jesus' teaching in Luke 11. Ask yourself, "Is my life as clean on the inside as I make it look on the outside? If Jesus looked inside the 'cup' of the Pharisees and saw greed and wickedness, what would He see in my life? How can I pursue a 'clean' life that is pleasing to God?"

Option #2:
Find a copy of the video or CD version of DC Talk's song "What If I Stumble?" from the *Jesus Freak* album (1995). Play the song and reflect on the honesty of the lyrics. Journal your responses. Be thankful for a "love that will never change," and pray for strength when your "walk becomes a crawl."

Bible Reference notes

Use these notes to deepen your understanding as you study the Bible on your own:

Luke 11:37-54

11:38 he was amazed. Like Simon in 7:39, Jesus' unorthodox actions raised silent questions in the mind of His host. *He did not first perform the ritual washing.* This had nothing to do with hygiene, but everything to do with religious tradition.

11:41 give ... then. They should repent of their greed and give to the poor instead. Such action would reflect a change of heart that would show inner cleanliness.

11:42 You give a tenth. The Old Testament required a tithe of garden and farm produce (Lev. 27:30-33; Deut. 14:22-29). Jesus attacks the Pharisees for holding fast to this (relatively) insignificant detail while they have totally neglected concerns like justice and love that dominate the Old Testament Law and prophets.

11:43 the front seat. The seats facing the congregation were the most important seats in the synagogue. To be seated there had become a sign of one's status in the congregation.

11:44 graves. Unmarked graves defile those who unknowingly come in contact with them (Num. 19:16).

11:46 load people with burdens. The scribes interpreted the law with a complex system of restrictions. Thus most felt condemned for their continual breaking of God's law. Jesus is incensed that the scribes assumed their duty stopped with interpreting the law. They made no attempt to help the people who struggled under the burden they created.

11:51 Abel. Abel was the first person to be murdered. It happened because his brother, like these leaders, refused to listen to God (Gen. 4:3-8). *Zechariah.* The context implies this was Zechariah (son of Jehoiada) who was murdered in the temple by people who refused to hear his word (2 Chron. 24:19-22).

11:52 taken away the key of knowledge! Instead of unlocking the Scriptures, the traditions of the scribes have securely locked away such knowledge from the people.

Session
10

LIFE IN SIN CITY: HOW DO I RESIST TEMPTATION?

Connections Prep

MAIN LIFEPOINT: Every one of us struggles with the temptation to do wrong things that hurt other people, God, or ourselves, but through our relationship with Christ and with the Holy Spirit's help we can train ourselves to resist.

To reinforce the LifePoint, leaders and small-group facilitators should understand the following more detailed CheckPoints and "Do" Points.

BIBLE STUDY CHECKPOINTS:
- Recognize that we are at war with unseen forces and we are all tempted
- Discover ways to resist falling into temptation
- Understand how Jesus and other Christ-followers function as our partners in the battles we face

LIFE CHANGE "DO" POINTS:
- Unleash the power of prayer in the fight against temptation
- Lock arms with an accountability partner to share our struggles
- Wield the sword of truth in our lives by studying, meditating on, and memorizing key Bible verses

PREPARATION:
- ☐ Review the *Leader's Book* for this session and prepare your teaching.
- ☐ Determine how you will subdivide students into small discussion groups.
- ☐ Recruit mature students or adults as small-group facilitators. Be sure these facilitators plan to attend.

REQUIRED SUPPLIES:
- ☐ *Essential Truth: Inviting Christ into My Reality* Leader books for each group facilitator
- ☐ *Essential Truth: Inviting Christ into My Reality* Student books for each student
- ☐ Pens or pencils for each student
- ☐ A bag of individually wrapped candy (for prizes)

10

 Get Ready

Read one of these short Bible passages each day, and focus on understanding the hero and the enemy in the larger story. Be sure to note what you discover and how it might affect you.

MONDAY

Read 1 Corinthians 10:12-13

Paul asserted that God won't allow us to be tempted beyond what we're able to withstand. But often temptation comes when we least expect it, making it more difficult to ignore. When was the last time you were caught off guard by a tempting thought or action? How did you overcome it? Or did you?

TUESDAY

Read Hebrews 4:15

Jesus was "tempted in every way." Is that surprising? What types of temptation do you think Jesus faced the most? Why? How does knowing that Jesus faced temptation add to His credibility as our Savior?

WEDNESDAY

Read Matthew 6:13

Asking God not to "lead us into temptation" seems odd. Do you think that God literally leads us into temptation? If not, where does temptation come from? (Check out James 1:12-17 and 1 Corinthians 7:5.)

THURSDAY

Read Genesis 3:1-3

In this passage, Satan appears as a serpent (remember the serpent didn't originally crawl on it's belly). Why a serpent? In what forms does Satan and evil present itself today?

FRIDAY

Read Genesis 3:4-5

The serpent's twisted spin on the fruit's ability to enlighten and empower was very tempting to Eve. If you could be a superhero with superpowers, what would they be? Would you want absolute power? Why or why not?

SATURDAY

Read Genesis 3:6-7

This passage opened a debate that has raged for millennia. Where did the fault belong: entirely on Eve who offered the fruit to Adam or was Adam to blame for his own sin? If someone presents a temptation to you and you cave in to it, who should take the blame: you or the person who introduced you to the temptation?

SUNDAY

Read Genesis 3:8-9

Literally and emotionally, Adam and Eve tried to hide from God. If God were to ask you the same question He the first couple in this passage, how would you respond?

LARGE-GROUP OPENING:
Get everyone's attention. Make announcements. Open your session with a prayer. Read the LifePoint to the students.

 LifePoint

Every one of us struggles with the temptation to do wrong things that hurt other people, God, or ourselves, but through our relationship with Christ and with the Holy Spirit's help we can train ourselves to resist.

Say What? *(15 MINUTES)*

SMALL-GROUP TIME:
Instruct students to separate into smaller groups of 4-8, preferably in a circle configuration. Call on the mature student or adult leaders you recruited to facilitate each small group through this "Say What?" segment.

Random Question of the Week:
Did Adam and Eve have bellybuttons? Why or why not?

Group Experience: Temptation Says ...

· Individually wrapped candies to award as prizes

Tell the group they are going to play a unique version of Simon Says. The catch is that instead of having to listen for the catch phrase "Simon Says" in order to know which orders to follow or skip, they must evaluate whether or not each command given is right or wrong. In other words, the instructions you give that are in no way rude, wrong, or inappropriate should be acted upon. Anything that isn't fully acceptable should be avoided. (The point is that some students will be tempted—largely for the sake of humor—to act on the "wrong" instructions just because they can. Or, they may fall prey to acting on a "wrong" instruction simply because they aren't paying attention.)

Ask your group to stand in a close circle, and then give the following commands. Should anyone act on a "wrong" request, ask him or her to sit down. Give the commands quickly.

· Compliment the person to your left   (OK)
· Smile and wave at the person directly across from you   (OK)
· Politely cover your mouth and cough   (OK)
· Tell the person across from you that his or her real name is "Stinky" (WRONG)
· Gently tug the hair of the person to your right   (WRONG)
· Quickly blink three times at anyone in the group   (OK)
· Politely cover your mouth and belch loudly   (WRONG)
· Slowly turn in a circle while humming *The Star Spangled Banner*   (OK)
· Shout, "You are a hedgehog!" to the person to your left.   (WRONG)

After the activity, give a piece of candy to everyone still standing, and then discuss the following questions:

1. . For some of you, it was very tempting to follow the "wrong" instructions just for the sake of getting a laugh or livening things up. In the real world, we are often

tempted to do the wrong thing for the sake of covering up mistakes or making ourselves look better. Can you think of some examples of how this is true?

2. Even if you managed to do all of the "right" things and none of the "wrong" in our game, you will sometimes mess up in life. Think about how you felt when a group member had to sit down for having done a "wrong" thing. How did you feel toward that person in their "failure"? How do you feel when a friend makes a poor moral choice?

3. How do you think God feels when we give into the temptation to rebel against Him? Why do you think He gave us the free will to make mistakes and poor choices?

LARGE-GROUP TIME: Have the students turn to face the front for this teaching time. Be sure you can make eye contact with each student in the room. Encourage students to follow along and take notes in their *Student Books*.

 # So What? *(30 MINUTES)*

Teaching Outline

I. Life in Sin City
    A. Ecclesiastes 1:9: "there is nothing new under the sun"
    B. Example: rapid growth of the pornography industry, but lust has always been there
    C. Temptation is always present in so many forms
    D. God never intended us to reach for things to pollute our minds & turn us away from Him

10

II. Genesis 3:1-9: How evil & pain broke into the world ... the "fall"
    A. Satan – fallen angel who rebelled against God in heaven
    B. Clever and crafty, the Devil—disguised as a serpent—brought rebellion to us
    C. Sin was here to stay
    D. Temptations of all kinds filled world & "good" became broken & distorted
    E. God didn't turn His back; He showed us the way and restore our relationship with Him

III. T-Shirt Philosophy
   A. "I know these two things: There is a God. And you are not Him."
   B. Common temptation: wanting to be God or at least to share His power

IV. The Way Out
   A. Jesus Himself could not avoid facing temptation while on earth (Hebrews)
   B. If Jesus has been through temptations we face & can show us the way out
   C. With Jesus & the Holy Spirit we can train ourselves to resist rebellion's pull

V. The Fight
   A. Resisting temptations always a struggle — we're at war with unseen forces
   B. As we fight to stay focused on God, temptations are launched at us
   C. Ephesians 6:11-12: At some point have to face temptations if you're ever going to defeat them
   D. Partners in the battle: Jesus our champion & close friends our support

Life in Sin City

Ecclesiastes 1:9 states "there is nothing new under the sun." And this is certainly true when it comes to temptation and our response to it. Consider, for example, the rapid growth of the pornography industry. In the 1700s, men struggled against and often succumbed to the temptation to lust at the sight of a lady's ankle as she modestly lifted her hem to descend from a carriage. By the 1900s, men had access to and many often visited street corner magazine stands overflowing with blatant pornography. Today, a tech-savvy student on an unfiltered computer can easily find pornography, dive into it, erase the "cookie" files, and never worry about getting caught. And what used to be a temptation reserved for men is quickly spreading to the female population as more and more women become addicted to pornographic images. The temptation has intensified, but lust has always tried to drag us down. "Why," some may wonder, "do people—even people who follow Jesus—fall into such habits and traps as viewing porn?"

People frequently submit to temptations of all varieties. ❶ <u>And even though we sometimes manage to avoid it, temptation is always present in so many forms</u>. Of course, God didn't design the world to be the way it is. He never intended for us to reach for things that would pollute our minds and turn us away from Him. ❷ <u>He began by creating the universe and all that is in it and calling it "good."</u> Humans, created in God's own image, especially received this declaration of total approval.

TEACHING FOR THE LARGE GROUP:
Share the "So What?" teaching with your students. You may modify it to fit your needs.

Be sure to highlight the underlined information, which gives answers to the *Student Book* questions and fill-in-the-blanks (shown in your margins)

❶ How prevalent is temptation in our world? Let's call out other areas in which we can be tempted!

❷ God didn't *design* the world the way it is. He began by creating the universe and all that is in it and calling it *good*.
't happen

❸ **Clever and crafty, the Devil, disguised as a serpent, convinced Eve to first doubt God's *words* and then His *heart* and *intentions*.**

❹ **Instead of turning His back on humanity when Adam and Eve gave into temptation, God began to …**
☐ **Let us live with our consequences**
☐ **Beat us up with guilt**
☐ **Pursue us with His redeeming love**
☐ **Overlook our rebellion and pretend it didn't happen**

❺ **In the person of *Jesus*, God showed us the way to restore our relationship with Him.**

Learning from the Bible …
Genesis 3:1-9

Ask for four volunteers to come to the front and read the parts of (1) the narrator, (2) Eve, (3) the serpent, and (4) God.

But Genesis 3:1-9 tells us the story of how evil and pain broke into history in a tragic episode known as "the fall." Satan, a fallen angel who rebelled against God in heaven, was quick to tempt mankind to rebel too. ❸ <u>Clever and crafty, the Devil (disguised as a serpent) convinced Eve to first doubt God's words and then His heart and intentions</u>. She made the choice to do what God said not to, Adam passively joined in, and the rest, they say, is history. Sin was here to stay as part of the human condition. From that moment on, temptations of all kinds filled the world and what started as "good" became broken and distorted.

❹ <u>But God didn't turn His back on Adam and Eve when their poor choices threatened to spoil His beautiful world. Instead, He pursued them—and thousands of generations of their children—with His redeeming love</u>. Eventually breaking into time Himself, ❺ <u>in the person of Jesus, God showed us the way and restore our relationship with Him</u>. But the Bible is clear that until Jesus returns to earth a second time, temptation is here to stay. So we must learn how to confront it, deal with it, and develop patterns in our lives that will help us to avoid, escape it, and overcome it.

Learning from the Bible

[NARRATOR] ¹ *Now the serpent was the most cunning of all the wild animals that the Lord God had made. He said to the woman, [SERPENT] "Did God really say, 'You can't eat from any tree in the garden'?"*
[NARRATOR] ² *The woman said to the serpent, [EVE] "We may eat the fruit from the trees in the garden. ³ But about the fruit of the tree in the middle of the garden, God said, 'You must not eat it or touch it, or you will die.' "*
[SERPENT] ⁴ *"No! You will not die. In fact, God knows that when you eat it your eyes will be opened and you will be like God, knowing good and evil." [NARRATOR] ⁶ Then the woman saw that the tree was good for food and delightful to look at, and that it was desirable for obtaining wisdom. So she took some of its fruit and ate [it], she also gave [some] to her husband, [who was] with her, and he ate [it]. ⁷ Then the eyes of both of them were opened, and they knew they were naked; so they sewed fig leaves together and made loincloths for themselves. ⁸ Then the man and his wife heard the sound of the Lord God walking in the garden at the time of the evening breeze, and they hid themselves from the Lord God among the trees of the garden. ⁹ So the Lord God called out to the man and said to him,*
[GOD] "Where are you?"

10

LARGE-GROUP TIME CONTINUED:
This is the meat of the teaching time. Remind students to follow along and take notes in their *Student Books*.

As you share the "So What?" information with students, make it your own. Use your natural teaching style.

Emphasize underlined information, which gives key points, answers to the *Student Book* questions or fill-in-the-blanks in the (shown in your margins).

❻ Jesus endured the temptations we face, and He successfully *resisted*. He can show us *the way out* of our temptations.

❼ What two things are we able to accomplish through a relationship with Jesus that are impossible without His help?
1) _____
2) _____

❽ According to the Apostle Paul, who or what is our war waged against? What are the enemy's weapons?

T-Shirt Philosophy

It's difficult to capture anything of real meaning off the back of a Christian t-shirt, but one particular shirt captures a very important truth: "I know these two things: There is a God. And you are not Him." In the Genesis account of the first sin, Eve fell victim to a now common temptation: wanting to be God or at least wanting to share in His power. Humans hunger for control and will often do anything to get it. We want to make our own decisions based on our own personal views of life and are many times willing to hurt others in the process. We want what will satisfy our needs, whims, and even our ugliest desires; and this tendency doesn't go away when we become Christ-followers. Many students have the mistaken idea that making a decision to trust their lives to Jesus will remove all sin and temptation from their lives. It just doesn't work that way!

The Way Out

We need to be as honest about the nature of our struggle as humans: Temptation is a constant companion—even in the lives of Christian believers. In fact, the author of Hebrews gives us our most comforting (and maybe also our most disturbing) teaching on temptation: Jesus Himself could not avoid facing temptation during His time on the earth. Of course, He was the only person ever to face temptation and walk away completely free and unscathed. **❻** But if Jesus has been through the temptations we face and yet resisted, He can show us the way out of our temptations. Since the fall, we have been born with the desire to rebel from God and do wrong. In fact, by our very nature, we are so full of rebellion that we have disconnected ourselves from God. **❼** But through a relationship with Jesus and with the Holy Spirit's help, there are two things we can accomplish: (1) we can train ourselves to resist rebellion's pull, and through Jesus' work of redemption, (2) we are able to approach God if we accept Jesus' payment for our failures and rebellion.

The Fight

Understand, however, that obeying God and resisting temptation do not come without a struggle. **❽** The Apostle Paul used battle imagery to communicate the war that we are at war with unseen forces. As we fight to stay focused on God, temptations are launched at us like flaming arrows. And Ephesians 6:11-12 reminds us to, "Put on the full armor of God so that you can stand against the tactics of the devil. For our battle is not against flesh and blood, but against the rulers, against the authorities, against the world powers of this darkness, against the spiritual forces of evil in the heavens."

Our Offensive Weapon

Two interesting truths are found in Paul's subsequent discussion of the armor of God. First, there is no mention of armor for our backsides. Turning and running is

⑨ We don't have to *invent* ways to resist temptation. Jesus and the Holy Spirit encourage us, strengthen us, and help us to fight against temptation using the power of *God's Word*!

⑩ Jesus is our advocate or *champion* who enables us to confess our issues to *God* and "approach the throne with *confidence*," so we can find *strength* in our struggles.

⑪ We cannot stand alone in struggles against temptation. We will find it helpful to have the support of a group of very close friends who can represent ...
☐ Cheerleaders who will keep us on track
☐ Jesus' influence in our lives
☐ The consequences of giving in to temptation

SMALL-GROUP TIME: Use this time to help students begin to integrate the truth they've learned into their lives . Small-group facilitators should lead the discussions and set the model for being open and honest in responding to questions

very wise when temptations threaten (e.g. Exodus 39:12), but at some point you're going to have to face your temptations if you are ever going to defeat them. The second is that we are given only one offensive weapon: the "sword of the Spirit which is God's word" (Ephesians 6:17). The author of Hebrews tells us how potent the Scriptures are in the hands of God's people: "Sharper than any two-edged sword, it penetrates even to dividing soul and spirit, joints and marrow" (Hebrews 4:12). **⑨** We don't have to invent ways to resist temptation. Jesus and the Holy Spirit encourage us, strengthen us, and help us to fight against temptation using the power of God's Word!

Partners in the Battle

Of course, without choosing to make Jesus the central partner in the struggles we face, we are helpless in the fight to guard our minds and hearts. But if we are in Jesus and He is in us (John 15:1-8), then He is always with us, and we can go to Him and share our struggles with Him. **⑩** He's our advocate or champion who enables us to confess our issues to God and "approach the throne with confidence," so that we can find strength in our struggles.

We are also wise to realize that wherever we go, there are others who will help to encourage us in the battle against temptation. **⑪** If you're going to be able to stand in the struggle against temptation, you simply cannot do it alone. You need the support of a few very close friends who will bring Jesus' influence in your life. With these friends, you can openly confess your struggles, honestly pray for those your friends face, and together you can lovingly hold one another accountable.

 Do What? *(15 MINUTES)* **10**

Personal Battles

1. What about the teaching on temptation most stood out to you? Were you surprised to learn that even Jesus faced temptation? Why do you think we often struggle to admit their own battles with wanting to do the wrong thing?

2. With which of the following areas of temptation do you most struggle?

☐ Lying or truth twisting

☐ Cheating

☐ Greed or selfishness

☐ Manipulation of others for personal gain or entertainment

☐ Substance Abuse

☐ Gossip

☐ Numbing out through TV, music, and other forms of media

☐ Lust

☐ Other: _____

☐ All of the Above

3. Which of the following do you need to focus on in your life in order to help you resist temptation? Mark all that apply.

☐ A closer relationship with Jesus

☐ A better understanding of what the Bible teaches about temptation

☐ A healthy prayer life in which you talk to God about your issues

☐ Accountability through another Christ-follower or a small group

☐ Other: _____

4. If you are comfortable sharing, give an example of how your relationship with Jesus has helped you overcome a specific temptation. How about your relationship with another person?

Small-group facilitators should reinforce the LifePoint for this session. Make sure that student's questions are invited and addressed honestly.

 LifePoint Review

Every one of us struggles with the temptation to do wrong things that hurt other people, God, or ourselves, but through our relationship with Christ and with the Holy Spirit's help we can train ourselves to resist.

Do" Points:

These "Do" Points will help you grab hold of this week's LifePoint. Be open and honest as you answer the questions within your small group.

1. <u>Unleash the power prayer in your fight against temptation.</u> Prayer is meant to be an honest pouring out of our hearts to God, but we often reduce it to a formal, stuffy speech said at meals or bedtime. Pastor John Piper says, "Prayer is a walkie-talkie for spiritual warfare, not a domestic intercom for our convenience." **When was the last time you talked to God about a specific struggle? How can you consistently make prayer your first response when confronted with temptation?**

2. <u>Lock arms with an accountability partner and share your struggles.</u> Laying down our pride and admitting our struggles and faults to other Christ-followers is difficult, but the cost is well worth knowing that we're not in the fight alone! **Do you have at least one other Christian friend with whom you can share openly and honestly about your struggles? If so, how often do you share and pray with that person?**

3. <u>Wield the sword of truth in your life</u> through studying, meditating on, and memorizing key Bible verses. Satan tempted Eve by manipulating words. As the old saying goes, "You have to stand for something, or you'll fall for everything." **Do you consistently spend time digging into God's truth, or do you have a weak understanding of the Bible? What steps can you take to make the Bible and prayer so much a part of your life that you instantly know what it has to say on a particular struggle?**

Prayer Connection:

"This is the time to encourage, support, and pray for each other in our journeys to admit our struggles to Jesus and to lean on Him for help.
Share prayer needs with the group, especially those related to overcoming temptation. Your group facilitator will close your time in prayer.

Prayer Needs:

Be sure to end your session by asking students to share prayer needs with one another, especially as they relate to issues brought up by today's session.

Encourage students to list prayer needs for others in their books so they can pray for one another during the week. Assign a student coordinator in each small group to gather the group's requests and e-mail them to the group members.

10

now What?

Encourage students to dig a little deeper by completing a "Now What" assignment before the next time you meet. Remind students about the "Are You Ready?" short daily Bible readings and related questions at the beginning of Session 11.

Remind them too that you care about them and are praying for their temptations!

Deepen your understanding of Jesus' power over temptation, and continue the journey you've begun today by choosing one of the following assignments to complete this week:

Option #1:
As you watch a favorite show and the commercials that interrupt it, list every temptation represented on the screen. Use the list as a first step in developing a "filter" by which you view media. Note that not all media is bad, but much of it leads you down a path that is damaging to you in the long run. Become increasingly aware of the messages that your viewing choices feed your mind and heart.

Option #2:
If you don't already have a small group or an accountability partner, make a list of at least five people you know who follow Jesus passionately. After praying for guidance, commit to asking one or more of those people how they deal with temptation. Discuss ways to battle against runaway thoughts and poor choices. See if they will get together sometime to talk about these things and pray together more. Move forward from there if and when God leads you both.

Option #3:
Give Scripture memorization a try. Find a verse or passage that applies to something you're dealing with. (You may need to use the concordance in the back of your Bible.) Then write that verse on a 3x5 card. Put it on the mirror in your bathroom or inside your locker. Concentrate on this one verse for a week and then ask yourself how it applies to your life. When you're ready, learn another.

Bible Reference notes

Use these notes to deepen your understanding as you study the Bible on your own:

Genesis 3:1-9

3:1 Did God really say, "You can't eat ... " God did not say this (2:16). Evil was ushered into the world because trust was broken. With one question, the serpent tempted Eve to distrust both God and her understanding of God's world.

3:3 You must not ... touch it. God had not said anything about touching the fruit; they were not to eat it (2:17). Eve did understand, however, that God had set a boundary that she was not to cross.

3:4 You will not die. Jesus said that lies were Satan's native tongue (John 8:44). In Eve's case, Satan's lie was in saying that God did not really mean what He said. Satan still uses that device today, trying to get people to water down, distrust, or discount God's words.

3:5 you will be like God. Satan made it sound to Eve like God was trying to hold onto a position and did not want anyone to become like Him. God was pictured as selfish. Satan still tries to twist God's words to make us believe things that are not true about Him.

3:6 good ... delightful ... desirable. Temptation has not changed over thousands of years. The New Testament describes the basic components of temptation as "the lust of the flesh, the lust of the eyes, and the pride in one's lifestyle" (1 John 2:16). Basically, Satan told Eve that the fruit would taste good (satisfy lust for food), that it looked good (temptation comes with the first look) and that it would make her wiser (improving her lifestyle). Satan uses the same tactics today to tempt people away from God. None of these outcomes, even if they seem realistic, are worth disregarding God's presence and power in our lives.

3:7 made loincloths for themselves. Adam and Eve had not gained great wisdom from the fruit; they had only succeeded in disobeying God and realizing the shame and guilt of that disobedience. With the advent of sin, everything looked different. Adam and Eve saw their own nakedness and looked for their own solution to the problem: making loincloths. But that was not a solution at all; covering themselves could not hide their disobedience or remove their guilt.

3:8 they hid. Adam and Eve foolishly tried to hide from the God who knew everything about them. The One who was the source of everything they needed was the One from whom they were hiding. Sin had disrupted their relationship with God. People still think that they can hide from God, but their efforts to do so are just as futile.

3:9 Where are you? God's goal is always to connect with us. He could have gone to where Adam and Eve were hiding, for He obviously knew where they were. However, He invited them to respond to Him. God immediately began to seek those who were lost.

Matthew 6:13

6:13 temptation. The request is not a plea to be exempt from the common moral struggles of life, but that God would empower the disciple to have the moral strength to resist giving in to evil during such struggles

1 Corinthians 10:13
10:13

10:13 Paul encourages the Corinthians to stand firm by reminding them that when Christians resist sin they do so in the knowledge that they will be able to endure. ***temptation.*** Paul has identified various temptations that Israel faced: the temptation of idolatry, the temptation to commit sexual immorality, the temptation to test God, and the temptation to grumble about where God led them. To be tempted is to be tested. Facing the choice of deserting God's will or doing God's will, the person must either resist or yield. Temptation is not sin. Yielding is. ***a way of escape.*** Temptation is not unusual or unexpected. Resisting it is not pleasant, but the Christian can do it with God's help.

Hebrews 4:15

4:15 tested in every way. Jesus was tempted in the desert by Satan (Luke 4:1-13). Here we find that He experienced every kind of temptation that we face. ***without sin.*** Technically, every high priest was without sin before offering atonement for the people. This was achieved by offering a sacrifice for himself prior to offering those for the people (5:3). Jesus was superior to the Old Testament priesthood because He had no sin for which to offer sacrifice.

NOTES

Session

THE GREAT PARADOX: WHAT MATTERS IN LIFE?

Connections Prep

MAIN LIFEPOINT: Life isn't pointless. We gain our lives and discover value and purpose when we give our lives away to Jesus.

To reinforce the LifePoint, leaders and small-group facilitators should understand the following more detailed CheckPoints and "Do" Points.

BIBLE STUDY CHECKPOINTS:
- Recognize that everyone searches for life's purpose and meaning
- Understand that committing our lives to Jesus is what makes them count
- Embrace the paradox of discovering true life by giving it away

LIFE CHANGE "DO" POINTS:
- Make Jesus our first priority
- Commit to giving our lives away for Jesus and to those who matter most to Him
- Develop a lifestyle of putting others first

PREPARATION:
☐ Review the *Leader's Book* for this session and prepare your teaching.
☐ Determine how you will subdivide students into small discussion groups.
☐ Recruit mature students or adults as small-group facilitators. Be sure these facilitators plan to attend.

REQUIRED SUPPLIES:
☐ *Essential Truth: Inviting Christ into My Reality* Leader books for each group facilitator
☐ *Essential Truth: Inviting Christ into My Reality* Student books for each student
☐ Pens or pencils for each student
☐ CD player
☐ Tim McGraw's song, "Live Like You Were Dying"
☐ Markers and a poster or tear sheet for each small group

 Get Ready

Read a Bible passage each day, get quiet, and let God speak to you. Be sure to jot down key ideas related to life priorities, meaning, and purpose.

MONDAY **Read Psalm 36:7-9**

As a joke, a man once tried to auction his soul online. What do you consider your most valuable possession? Is there anything in your life that you simply would not put a price on?

TUESDAY **Read James 1:17-18**

Jesus' brother explained that God is the source of everything good. While we often spend time worrying about the negatives in our lives, we need to focus on the positives. What "good gifts" has God given you?

WEDNESDAY **Read John 14:6-7**

It has been said that one word, "the," got Jesus killed. It wasn't His claim that He was *a* savior that got Him crucified; it was His teaching that he was *the* way, *the* truth, and *the* life. Do you believe there is more than one way to God? Why do you believe it? How do you communicate this belief to others, or do you try to altogether avoid the subject of Jesus' identity?

THURSDAY **Read Matthew 6:26**

God is the intelligent designer behind all we see in nature. If He could carve mountain ranges in a day and create thousands of different fascinating animals in another, we can trust Him to take care of our needs. So why do you struggle with worry?

FRIDAY

Read Galatians 5:22-26

Paul describes what should come out of the life of a true follower of Jesus. Just as we should get orange juice when we squeeze an orange, we should see attributes and characteristics reflecting Jesus' when a Christ-follower is placed under pressure. When life squeezes you, what usually comes out? How does your answer compare to the list that Paul provides?

SATURDAY

Read Ephesians 2:4-9

When our court system convicts a person and assigns the death sentence, that individual is often referred to as a "dead man walking." That phrase well describes our fate if we remain separated from God. What saves us from the death sentence?

SUNDAY

Read Luke 9:23-27

A paradox is when the truth is opposite of what seems logical (or it's 2 doctors). How did Jesus turn the world upside down (or right side up again) by demonstrating the great paradox in His own life?

LARGE-GROUP OPENING:
Get everyone's attention.
Make announcements.
Open your session with a prayer. Read the LifePoint to the students.

 LifePoint

Life isn't pointless. We gain our lives and discover value and purpose when we give our lives away to Jesus.

11

Say What? *(15 MINUTES)*

SMALL-GROUP TIME:
Before dividing the class into groups, ask everyone to listen carefully to the words of Tim McGraw's song, "Live Like You Were Dying." Play the CD for the entire group.

Then instruct students to separate into smaller groups of 4-8, preferably in a circle configuration. Call on the mature student or adult leaders you recruited to facilitate each small group through the "Say What?" segment.

Random Question of the Week:

If frankfurters are made of beef, pork, or a combination of both, why are they called "hot *dogs*"?

Group Experience: Live Like You Were Dying

- CD player
- Tim McGraw's song, "Live Like You Were Dying"
- Markers and a poster board or tear sheet

In 2004, country singer Tim McGraw had a crossover radio hit entitled, "Live Like You Were Dying." In the song, a man is diagnosed with a condition that gives him only a few months to live. As a result, he experiences things he never dreamed of doing. He goes skydiving, tries bull riding, and chooses to forgive those who he'd long refused to pardon.

This powerful song was written in memory of his famous baseball star father, "Tug" McGraw. "Tug," whom Tim didn't meet until he was 11, died of brain cancer at the age of 59. For the last several months of his life, Tug moved in with Tim and his family in their Tennessee home. They shared stories and experiences, knowing Tug's time on this earth was coming to an end."[1]

1. As a small group, brainstorm 10 things you'd want to be sure to do if you were told your lives were going to suddenly end within six months. Write your lists on a poster or tear sheet.

2. If everyone will die someday, what's the purpose of living?

3. What keeps us from doing the things we listed in question 1? How would our feelings change if we really did find out we have a limited time to live?

4. What from this life can we take into the next? How should that knowledge affect what we do while here on earth?

After giving students a few minutes to work, ask the following:

Read aloud several of the items the students listed on their tear sheet.

So What? *(30 MINUTES)*

LARGE-GROUP TIME:
Have the students turn to face the front for this teaching time. Be sure you can make eye contact with each student in the room. Encourage students to follow along and take notes in their *Student Books*.

Teaching Outline

I. The God-Shaped Hole
A. French philosopher Jean Paul Sartre: that each human is born with "a God-shaped hole"
B. Being left unfilled, we become vacuum for all kinds of nonsense in the name of spirituality
C. We are all created with an emptiness that only a relationship with God can fill
D. We'll never find true satisfaction & joy until we accept a relationship with Jesus & live for Him.
E. Why do we exist?
   1. Finding our identity
   2. Connecting with our mission
   3. Becoming all that God created us to be

II. Luke 9: 23-27

III. Living Life on Purpose
A. Pastor Rick Warren's *The Purpose-Driven Life*: explains how we can live for God's eternal purposes instead of for ourselves
B. Ashley Smith convinced Brian Nichols not to kill her & surrender because God still had a plan for his life

IV. Giving Up Your Life to Find It
A. Discover true meaning when we give our lives away to Jesus & to what matters most to Him - hurting people
B. Faced with a choice: choose LIFE with Jesus Christ or DEATH without Him
C. Confessing & believing in Jesus (Rom. 10:9-10) open door to a restored relationship with God
D. Join Him on His mission to "seek and save the lost" (Luke 19:10).
E. All people searching for purpose & meaning; most go about this in the wrong way

11

TEACHING FOR THE LARGE GROUP:
Share the "So What?" teaching with your students. You may modify it to fit your needs.

Be sure to highlight the underlined information, which gives answers to the *Student Book* questions and fill-in-the-blanks (shown in your margins)

❶ According to Jean Paul Sartre, each human is born with a *God-shaped hole*.

❷ The emptiness of the "hole" can only be filled through …
☐ Giving to charities
☐ Collecting expensive "toys"
☐ Relationship with God
☐ Pouring out our lives for others

❸ We'll never find true *satisfaction* and *joy* until we accept a relationship with Jesus and commit to *living* for Him.

❹ What is the point of a person's existence?

V. God Comes to Us and Invites Us to Join Him

A. Christianity amazing distinctive from other world religions: GRACE

B. We don't serve God in order to "get in good" with Him

C. Only three things that will last throughout eternity

    1. Word of God

    2. The church of Jesus Christ

    3. People.

D. For a life that matters forever, join God in His mission of rescuing people from darkness!

The God-Shaped Hole

From his research and personal observation, French ❶ philosopher Jean Paul Sartre surmised that each human is born with "a God-shaped hole" that, by virtue of being left unfilled, has become a vacuum for all kinds of nonsense in the name of spirituality. Sartre probably wasn't the first to propose this idea that ❷ we are all created with an emptiness that only a relationship with God can fill, but he got credit for stating it in these terms.

If you think about it, the theory makes a lot of sense. We've all seen people frantically trying to make their lives count by giving huge amounts of stuff to every disaster relief and charity fund that asks for help. Others become consumed by filling their lives with success and wealth: bigger houses, bigger toys, more money, more respect. But ultimately, it doesn't matter what people try to fill their voids with. Like the critical last piece to a jigsaw puzzle, God is the only thing that can fill in the gap. While we all instinctively search for meaning and even purpose, ❸ we'll never find true satisfaction and joy until we accept a relationship with Jesus and commit to living for Him.

So why do we exist? Why are we here? Jesus came to show by His life and mission that anything short of giving your life to God will not satisfy your quest for meaning in life. In fact, ❹ finding our identity, connecting with our mission, becoming all that God created us to be is the whole point of our existence. Today we're going to explore some of Jesus' teachings that at first seem paradoxical, but hold the keys for living a life that matters.

Learning from
the Bible ...

Luke 9: 23-27

You may read the
passage yourself or
ask a volunteer to
come to the front of
the room and read it.

Learning from the Bible

23 Then [Jesus] said to [them] all, "If anyone wants to come with, he must deny himself, take up his cross daily, and follow Me. 24 For whoever wants to save his life will lose it, but whoever loses his life because of Me will save it. 25 What is a man benefited if he gains the whole world, yet loses or forfeits himself? 26 For whoever is ashamed of Me and My words, the Son of Man will be ashamed of him when He comes in His glory and that of the Father and the holy angels. 27 I tell you the truth: there are some standing here who will not taste death until they see the kingdom of God."

Living Life on Purpose

**LARGE-GROUP TIME
CONTINUED:**
This is the meat of the
teaching time. Remind
students to follow along
and take notes in their
Student Books.

As you share the
"So What?" information
with students, make
it your own. Use your
natural teaching style.

Emphasize underlined
information, which gives
key points, answers to
the *Student Book*
questions or fill-in-the-
blanks in the (shown in
your margins).

In the early 1990's, Pastor Rick Warren released a book entitled *The Purpose-Driven Life*. In this book, Warren used Scripture to tell people that they were created with a purpose. In simple, straightforward language he explained how they could live for God's eternal purposes instead of for themselves. One of the most powerful stories to come from the impact of *The Purpose-Driven Life* included two people desperate to find meaning in their lives.

Ashley Smith was headed out of her apartment when the subject of an intense Atlanta-area wide manhunt, Brian Nichols, aimed his loaded gun at her and forced her back into the apartment complex. Only hours before, Nichols had gone on a killing spree that left at least three dead. Instead of growing hysterical, Smith held her composure and decided to reach out to the man. She talked with Nichols, listened to his story, and shared her own struggles as a former drug abuser whose life had been less than perfect. She read to Nichols from chapter 33 of *The Purpose-Driven Life*, which centers on the idea that in every moment there is a chance to serve others. Hours later, Smith convinced Nichols to surrender to authorities because God still had a plan for his life.

Theirs was such an amazing story of grace that even the writer for a major news magazine couldn't get over it: "He was an alleged rapist and murderer. She was tied up in a bathtub, clinging to the wreckage of a life that was barely afloat. One was a monster, the other a woman unable to care for her 5-year-old .... And out of that came something, well, beautiful. He saw his purpose: to serve God in prison, to turn his life around ... She saw hers: to make that happen. These people weren't saints"[2]

11

Giving Up Your Life to Find It

How do you make sense of a story like that? How do you explain this seemingly random journey we call life? Why are you here at all? Questions like this lead back to one consistent and compelling answer. ❺ True meaning is discovered when we give our lives away to Jesus and also to the things that matter most to Him: hurting people. As one theologian noted, there are at least two breathlessly beautiful movements in God's plan to bring the whole world back into close relationship with Him through His Son. The first is God's grace in bringing us to Jesus in the first place. God continues to put you in places, situations, and conversations in which you come face to face with the reality that your own life is broken, and you cannot fix it on your own. ❻ You are faced with a choice: choose life through God's grace by faith in Jesus Christ, or choose death by trusting in yourself. Confessing with our mouths and believing with our hearts in Jesus (Romans 10:9-10) open the door to a restored relationship with God, and the second movement in the symphony of life begins. That second movement is the opportunity to give your life away to God for the purpose of joining Him on His mission to "seek and save the lost" (Luke 19:10).

By now, you should instinctively recognize that all people are searching for purpose and meaning. Early in life (especially during our teen years), we are driven to experiment with temporary pleasures that we hope will bring us satisfaction. Most of us learn that there is some connection between meaning and helping others. Unfortunately, most people who aren't in a relationship with Jesus go about this in the wrong way. They forget that we are made in God's image (Genesis 1:26-27), we are all His children (1 John 3:1), and we are of worth to Him (Matthew 6:26). ❼ By their own effort, they try to build meaningful relationships, help in acts of service, or give of their time and resources in attempt to feel better about their lives. This tendency, in fact, is the basis behind many world religions.

God Comes to Us and Invites Us to Join Him

But one of the amazing truths about Christianity that is different from all other world religions is that it is the only belief system in which God comes to us. Every other religion teaches that there are things you have to do, laws you must obey, pilgrimages you must make, and behaviors you must practice in order to get to God on your own. The Bible teaches the opposite! We are unable to please God or pay a price sufficient for our failures and mistakes. So by His grace, God sent Jesus to give us life by giving His away. It is at the cross where Jesus gave His life away, that you discover that giving your life away to Jesus is the key to making your life count. ❽ We don't serve God in order to "get in good" with Him; instead, we serve out of a response to His tenderness and unbelievable mercy. It is out of this over-

❺ True meaning is discovered when we do what two things?

1) _____

2) _____

❻ Everyone is given the choice to choose *life* through God's grace by faith in Jesus Christ, or to choose *death* by trusting in themselves.

❼ What tendency is the basis behind many world religions?

❽ Why should we serve others?

flow of God's love for us that we have the motivation, the desire, and the ability to give our lives away in the service of Jesus. ❾ There are only three things that will last throughout eternity: the Word of God, the church of Jesus Christ, and people. If you want to make your life matter forever, it makes sense to join God in His mission of rescuing people from darkness!

 # Do What? *(15 MINUTES)*

A Great Paradox

1. Can you think of an example of how someone might save his life by losing it? If so, explain. How does that illustration help you understand how dedicating your life to living for Jesus "saves" it?

2. In today's passage, Jesus taught that if we want to live for Him, we must "take up our cross" and "follow" Him. What does that mean?

3. What is the purpose statement for your life? Why is it important that you have one?

 # LifePoint Review

Life isn't pointless. We gain our lives and discover value and purpose when we give our lives away to Jesus.

"Do" Points:

These "Do" Points will help you grab hold of this week's LifePoint. Risk being open and honest as you answer the questions within your small group.

SMALL-GROUP TIME: Use this time to help students begin to integrate the truth they've learned into their lives while they connect with the other students in the group, the leaders, and with God.

Ask students to divide back into small groups and discuss the "Do What?" questions. Small-group facilitators should lead the discussions and set the model for being open and honest in responding to questions.

Small-group facilitators should reinforce the LifePoint for this session. Make sure that student's questions are invited and addressed honestly.

11

1. <u>Make Jesus your first priority.</u> The first item in the "Westminster Catechism" is still as true today as ever: *"The chief end (purpose) of man is to glorify God and enjoy Him forever."* It's easy to get so busy that we forget to pray and spend time with God, but He wants to be our first priority.
What steps can you take to make sure that God isn't just getting the leftovers of your time?

2. <u>Commit to giving your life away for Jesus and to those who matter most to Him.</u> Most people prefer to ignore the thousands of elderly people resigned to spending their last days alone in nursing homes. People get too busy to remember that others ache with hunger, secret fears, and loneliness.
What are some ways you can share the love of Jesus with the hurting people in your community?

3. <u>Develop a lifestyle of putting others first.</u> It's easy to get in the habit of thinking only for ourselves. But Jesus wants us to be considerate of others, and He wants us to be willing to put their needs above our own.
How can you live out this idea in your home? With your friends? In your school? In your church?

Prayer Connection:

This is the time to encourage, support, and pray for each other in our journeys to grasp God's purpose for us. Share prayer needs with the group, especially those related to knowing and doing what Jesus would have you do with your life. Your group facilitator will close your time in prayer.

Prayer Needs:

Be sure to end your session by asking students to share prayer needs with one another, especially as they relate to issues brought up by today's session.

Encourage students to list prayer needs for others in their books so they can pray for one another during the week. Assign a student coordinator in each small group to gather the group's requests and e-mail them to the group members.

now What?

Encourage students to dig a little deeper by completing a "Now What" assignment before the next time you meet. Remind students about the "Are You Ready?" short daily Bible readings and related questions at the beginning of Session 12.

Remind students that God has created them with a special mission and He wants them on His team!

Deepen your understanding of who God is, and continue the journey you've begun today by, choosing one of the following assignments to complete this week:

Option #1:

Keep a time log of your week. After a week, evaluate how you're spending your days. How much of time is dedicated to doing things that honor God and encourage others? Ask God to help you, and then fill in your calendar with specific prayer and ministry appointments designed to give Jesus a greater portion of your time.

Option #2:

Plan to meet a need. Find someone within your circle of influence who could benefit from encouragement. For instance, make time to visit an elderly neighbor who is lonely and forgotten. Help him or her by taking care of basic household needs, listening to stories, and sharing your own.

Option #3:

Consider giving a semester or summer to missions work. Use the Web as a research tool, exploring missions projects and assignments available to students such as Youth With A Mission (*www.ywam.org*), Teen Mission (*www.teenmissions.org*), International Mission Board (*www.imb.org*), the North American Mission Board (*www.studentz.com*), General Board of Global Missions (*www.gbgm-umc.org*), Young Life (*www.younglife.org*), Campus Crusade for Christ (*www.campuscrusade.com*), and the Billy Graham Evangelistic Association (*www.passageway.org*). Be sure you check the Web pages for your church and denominational missions.

11

Bible Reference Notes

Use these notes to deepen your understanding as you study the Bible on your own:

Luke 9:23-27

9:23 come with Me. This is to take on the role of a disciple, one committed to the teachings of a master. ***deny himself.*** This is to no longer live with self-satisfaction as the primary aim of life. Self must be denied in favor of doing the will of God. ***take up his cross.*** It is a metaphor emphasizing the call for all Jesus' disciples to put aside one's own desires and interests out of loyalty to Jesus. ***daily.*** Luke alone includes this. Following Jesus is a day-by-day commitment.

9:26 Comes in His glory! While His present suffering is real, the future glory of the Son of Man is pictured here (Dan. 7:13-14)

Matthew 6:26

6:26 worth more than they. This does not denigrate the importance of animals to God. It is because humanity has a special relationship and responsibility to the Creator that people (made in God's image and given dominion over the creation—Gen. 1) are "more valuable" than animals.

John 14:6

14:6 I am the way. The destination to which Jesus is going is not so much a place, but a person—the Father (7:33; 8:21). The way for the disciples to come to the Father is through the Son, who, by His death, opens the way for them (Heb. 10:19-22)

Ephesians 2:4-9

2:4 abundant. Paul makes more allusions to "riches" in Ephesians than anywhere else in his writings. ***mercy.*** Not only love, but also mercy motivates God. Love and mercy are closely related. ***because of His great love.*** Love is God's reason for rescuing fallen humanity (Deut. 7:6-9). This is one of four words that Paul uses to explain God's motivation for reaching out to humanity: love, mercy, grace, and kindness.

2:5 made us alive. Paul coins this phrase to describe exactly what happens to us when we are "in Christ"; namely, we share in Christ's resurrection, ascension, and enthronement. ***By grace.*** This resurrection from spiritual death cannot be earned. It is simply given. Grace is God's unmerited favor or gift to us.

2:8 For by grace you are saved. This is the second time Paul acclaims this amazing fact (v. 5). ***through faith.*** Salvation does not come about because of faith in and of itself. Salvation comes by grace (from God) through faith (from us).

2:8-9 not from yourselves ... not from works. Salvation is not a reward for being good or keeping the Law.

1 Accessed 9/19/05 from http://archive.parade.com/2004/0822_tim_mcgraw.html.
2 "When Grace Arrives Unannounced," Time Magazine, March 28, 2005.

Session

12

MAY THE FORCE BE WITH YOU: WHAT'S UP WITH THE HOLY SPIRIT?

Connections Prep

MAIN LIFEPOINT: The Holy Spirit isn't a mystical force. He is the active third person of the Trinity who gives power and direction to every true Christ-follower and the church.

To reinforce the LifePoint, leaders and small-group facilitators should understand the following more detailed CheckPoints and "Do" Points.

BIBLE STUDY CHECKPOINTS:
- Examine the Holy Spirit's identity and learn about His characteristics
- Understand how the Holy Spirit impacted the early church
- Explore ways the Holy Spirit empowers and equips us on our journey with Jesus

LIFE CHANGE "DO" POINTS:
- Accept the Holy Spirit as our guide who desperately wants to help us and empower us to live the amazing lives God the Father intended for each of us.
- Embrace the unique roles in the larger story for which the Holy Spirit has gifted each of us
- Develop our gifts through the Holy Spirit's direction and power

PREPARATION:
- ☐ Review the *Leader's Book* for this session and prepare your teaching.
- ☐ Determine how you will subdivide students into small discussion groups.
- ☐ Recruit mature students or adults as small-group facilitators. Be sure these facilitators plan to attend.

REQUIRED SUPPLIES:
- ☐ *Essential Truth: Inviting Christ into My Reality* Leader books for each group facilitator
- ☐ *Essential Truth: Inviting Christ into My Reality* Student books for each student
- ☐ Pens or pencils for each student
- ☐ A Lite Brite toy and Lite Brite pegs for each small group (Ask around. Lots of these are stored in closets.) **Note:** The new Lite Brite (created by Hasbro®) can be purchased at several stores
- ☐ Piece of black construction paper for each small group

12

 Get Ready

Read one of these short Bible passages each day to find out who the Holy Spirit really is. Be sure to jot down any insights the Holy Spirit reveals about Himself each day.

MONDAY

Read John 14:25-27

When Jesus told His disciples He would soon be leaving earth, He promised the Holy Spirit would come to give them peace. How do you think they reacted to this news? Why was it important for someone to still be with them? How could the gift of peace benefit you right now?

TUESDAY

Read Romans 8:22-27

Paul tells us that the Holy Spirit helps us connect with God. Have you ever have a hard time putting your thoughts and feelings into words and had someone help you out? How does it feel to have someone express just what you are feeling but can't express?

WEDNESDAY

Read Acts 13:1-4

Some people claim to hear voices. Others claim to hear God's. Still others have compelling mental impressions. How does God usually speak to you? How would you like Him to speak to you? How do you think the Holy Spirit spoke to these early leaders in the church?

THURSDAY

Read 1 Corinthians 2:6-16

Paul shares why it is important to have the Holy Spirit's help for navigating life. Do you know two people who are so close that they can finish each other's sentences? How is the relationship between God and the Holy Spirit like that?

FRIDAY

Read 1 Corinthians 12:1-11

The Holy Spirit plays an important role in the unity of God's people. How does a sports team benefit from having a great coach who understands each person's role? How does the Holy Spirit function like a coach? Why does unity even matter?

SATURDAY

Read Ephesians 4:29-32

When was the last time you let down or disappointed someone you respect? Do you think God cares when we fail? Is it possible to let down the Holy Spirit with our attitudes or actions?

SUNDAY

Read Acts 2:1-13

Describe the most exciting moment in your life up to this point. Have you ever experienced anything so amazing it was beyond words? How would you have reacted to what happened to the disciples in this passage?

LARGE-GROUP OPENING:
Get everyone's attention. Make announcements. Open your session with a prayer. Read the LifePoint to the students.

 LifePoint

The Holy Spirit isn't a mystical force. He is the active third person of the Trinity who gives power and direction to every true Christ-follower and the church.

12

SMALL-GROUP TIME:
Instruct students to separate into smaller groups of 4-8, preferably in a circle configuration. Call on the mature student or adult leaders you recruited to facilitate each small group through this "Say What?" segment.

Say What? *(15 MINUTES)*

Random Question of the Week:

What animal would make the weirdest house pet?

Group Experience: Plugged In

Option #1 (IF you can locate some Lite Brite toys at a toy or department store):

- · A Lite Brite toy and colored Lite Brite pegs
- · Piece of black construction paper

Tell the group that they need to make a clown's face on their Lite Brite panel. Attach the black piece of construction paper to the toy's face. Then give each student an equal number of colored pegs. Tell them that they cannot plug the toy in until the picture is complete. For 5-7 minutes, allow the students to work together. Do not allow one or two people to take charge; make it a group effort.

Say something like, "The goal in making Lite Brite art is to create a picture using a lot of simple plastic pegs. It's similar to a type of art known as mosaic, in which an artist uses thousands of tiny colored shards of ceramic and glass to create a larger image."

Plug in the Lite Brite so that the image is revealed. Then discuss the following questions:

Option #2 (IF you can't locate or purchase some Lite Brite toys):

- · Markers or crayons for each student
- · A poster board or tear sheet for each small group

Tell the group that you want them to work together to draw (on their poster board or tear sheet) a circus clown riding an elephant. Here's the catch: Let them know you're going to turn the lights off just before they begin. Be sure it's a full group effort.

After a couple of minutes turn the lights back on and allow the teams to laugh at their creations. Allow a couple more minutes to let the teams salvage their drawings. Then discuss the following questions:

Option #1: (use questions below)

Until we plugged in the toy, we had only a basic idea of how our picture would look and from what we could tell—our picture wasn't very exciting. Our lives and the church have a power source as well that truly makes a difference when it comes to capturing the hearts and attention of the world.

Option #2: (use questions below)

Without the power on, we were working in the dark, with no idea what we were really creating and the result wasn't very exciting or successful. When we connected with the power source, the picture and our work became much more clear and effective. Our lives and the church have a power source as well that truly makes a difference when it comes to capturing the hearts and attention of the world.

1. Any idea what our real power source is?

2. Who exactly is the Holy Spirit? In what way does He serve as a "power source" for Christ-followers? How is trying to do life without His help like trying to finish a picture without plugging in the light?

3. Why do you think the mention of the Holy Spirit make some people—including Christians—uncomfortable?

 # So What? *(30 MINUTES)*

LARGE-GROUP TIME: Have the students turn to face the front for this teaching time. Be sure you can make eye contact with each student in the room. Encourage students to follow along and take notes in their *Student Books*.

Teaching Outline

I. Embracing the Mystery

    A. Understanding the Trinity is still one of the great mysteries of life

    B. Most often confused about the Holy Spirit's role

        1. Holy Spirit is simply hard to explain

        2. Hundreds of references to Him, His nature, & His work in Bible

        3. Holy Spirit equal partner with God the Father & God the Son (a person, not a force)

        4. Spirit serves as a Helper, Counselor, & Source of hope & strength to Christ-followers

12

II. Acts 2:1-13

III. Plugging into the Power

 A. Memories of North American blackout of 2003

 B. Power outages in our spiritual lives

  1. World decayed by the effects of evil weakens our resolve with Jesus

  2. Holy Spirit deeply loves us & wants to serve as our constant helper

  3. Spiritual power shortage leaves us feeling helpless & alone

 C. Jesus promised to send the Holy Spirit in His name (John 14:26-27)

  1. To continue the work He had begun

  2. To fuel the church for its worldwide mission

  3. So the disciples did not have to fear Jesus' leaving; we can be confident of God's help

IV. The Holy Spirit

 A. Jesus instructed them to stay in Jerusalem until they were "clothed with power"

 B. When Spirit made His presence known to the first Christians with "a sound like that of a violent rushing wind" (Acts 2:2)

 C. "Tongues of fire" - Throughout the Scripture, fire is a symbol of God's presence

 D. Our God is a "consuming fire" (Hebrews 12:29)

  1. Spirit fans the flame of that fire in heart of every person who truly seeks to follow Him

  2. Book of Acts all about how Spirit works to overcome obstacles to faith in Jesus

  3. Within just a few decades church moved from a few dozen scared & confused followers to become the greatest movement of God the world had ever seen!

  4. Power from personal care & awesome fire of Holy Spirit drawing people to light

 E. Holy Spirit helps believers in the same amazing ways today

  1. Gives abilities we can use to serve God & others (1 Cor. 12, Rom. 12, and Eph. 4)

  2. As the "Counselor" — helps teach us what we need to know

  3. Guide — "guide you into all truth" (John 16:12-13) & in decisions (2 Cor. 2:10)

  4. We worship in "spirit and in truth" (John 4:24)

  5. Brings about unity in the church (Acts 10:34-35)

**TEACHING FOR THE
LARGE GROUP:**

❶ **God, Jesus, and
the Holy Spirit are
distinct yet *separate*
persons of the *Trinity*.**

❷ **Which of the
following best
describes the Holy
Spirit's relationship
with God and Christ?**
☐ **Equal partner**
☐ **Apprentice**
☐ **Superior**
☐ **Invisible life force**

❸ **To those who
accept relationship
with Jesus, the Holy
Spirit serves as *Helper*,
Counselor, and Source
of *hope* and *strength*.**

**Learning from
the Bible ...**

Acts 2:1-13

**You may read the
passage yourself or
ask a volunteer to
come to the front of the
room and read it.**

What People Believe About God

Let's face it, understanding how **❶** <u>God, Jesus, and the Holy Spirit are distinct yet separate persons of the Trinity</u> is still one of the great mysteries of life. We get it ... kind of, but God is so far beyond us that it's still not fully clear to us. Even when we research Scripture, try to wrap our minds around commentary offered on the subject, and discuss everything we can about them, there are times when we simply come up short in explaining how they function. Even well-intentioned Bible teachers have tried to explain the relationships between the members of the Trinity without success. While most people can grasp God as Father and Creator and Jesus as Son and Redeemer, they often get confused about the Holy Spirit's role.

The reality is that the Holy Spirit is simply hard to explain. But the Bible, especially in the New Testament, gives us hundreds of references to Him, His nature, and His work. Through vivid accounts, we see that **❷** <u>the Holy Spirit is an equal partner with God the Father and God the Son</u> **❸** <u>who serves as a Helper, Counselor, and Source of hope and strength to those who accept a relationship with Jesus</u>.

But what does that really mean? Today we'll look at one Bible account of how the Holy Spirit chooses to work as we seek to understand more about the Holy Spirit's vital role in our lives.

Learning from the Bible

¹ When the day of Pentecost had arrived, they were all together in one place. ² Suddenly a sound like that of a violent rushing wind came from heaven, and it filled the whole house where they were staying. ³ And tongues, like flames of fire that were divided, appeared to them and rested on each one of them. ⁴ Then they were all filled with the Holy Spirit and began to speak in different languages, as the Spirit gave them ability for speech.

⁵ There were Jews living in Jerusalem, devout men from every nation under heaven. ⁶ When this sound occurred, the multitude came together and was confused because each one heard them speaking in his own language. ⁷ And they were astounded and amazed, saying, "Look, aren't all these who are speaking Galileans? ⁸ How is it that we hear, each of us, in our own native language? ⁹ Parthians, Medes, Elamites; those who live in Mesopotamia, in Judea and Cappadocia, Pontus and Asia, ¹⁰ Phrygia and Pamphylia, Egypt and the parts of Libya near Cyrene; visitors from Rome, both Jews and proselytes, ¹¹ Cretans and Arabs—we hear them speaking in our own languages the magnificent acts of God." ¹² And they were all astounded and perplexed, saying to one another, "What could this be?" ¹³ But some sneered and said, "They're full of new wine!"

12

LARGE-GROUP TIME CONTINUED:
This is the meat of the teaching time. Remind students to follow along and take notes in their *Student Books*.

As you share the "So What?" information with students, make it your own. Use your natural teaching style. You may modify it with your own perspectives and teaching needs. Emphasize the underlined information, which gives key points, answers to the *Student Book* questions or fill-in-the-blanks in the (shown in your margins).

❹ Without the Holy Spirit's influence, Christ-followers would face a spiritual *power shortage* that would leave us feeling *helpless* and *alone*.

❺ At what moment were the early Christ-followers "clothes with power" as Jesus promised?
☐ When Jesus went back to heaven
☐ When God said, "Now!"
☐ When the Holy Spirit came down with the sound of a violent wind

Plugging into the Power

During the middle of a heat wave in 2003, much of the Northeastern United States and Canada experienced a blackout that lasted several days. Across the region, businesses closed, mass transit halted, and grocers gave away more ice cream than people could eat because it was melting in freezers that didn't work. Amazing aerial shots showed thousands of New York City workers forced to walk home in a mass exodus down city streets and bridges. Some people walked 12 hours just to get home! In the investigation that followed, it was discovered that there were several old, weak systems linked into the complex power grid that served that part of the United States. When they failed, it set off a chain reaction that left 50 million people without power[1]!

We often see power shortages in our spiritual lives that compare to this scenario. The challenge of following Christ in a world decayed by the effects of evil can weaken our resolve to stay in close relationship with Him. That's where the Holy Spirit comes in. He is not just an impersonal force or power source. He deeply loves us and wants to serve as our counselor, guide, and constant source of help. ❹ Without His active involvement, we too would experience a spiritual power shortage that would leave us feeling helpless and alone.

While the Spirit was present in Old Testament times (Exodus 3:1-6, Zechariah 4:6), it was Jesus Himself who promised His followers that the Father would send the Holy Spirit in His name to continue the work He had begun and to fuel the church for its worldwide mission (John 14:26-27). Because of this, the disciples did not have to fear Jesus' leaving, and as believers today we can be confident that we have God's help for our journey.

The story we read from Acts 2 describes an event that occurred right after Jesus' death. His followers were hiding out, scared, and scattered. Even after Jesus' resurrection appearances, they were filled with awe and wonder at all that had happened, but they were still uncertain and didn't have a plan for sharing the good news of Jesus' resurrection with the world. While Jesus gave them that plan (Matthew 29:18-20, Luke 24:47-49), ❺ He instructed them to stay in Jerusalem until they were "clothed with power." Luke describes the moment when that happened: when the Spirit made His presence known to the first Christians with "a sound like that of a violent rushing wind" (Acts 2:2).

If we are going to grasp the transforming power of the moment, then we must put ourselves in the sandals of the early church people and imagine how the Holy Spirit impacted the early church. We noticed in the passage that the Holy Spirit descended on these Christ-followers in "tongues like flames of fire."

6 It's significant that the Holy Spirit first appeared to Jesus' followers in the form of fire because fire is a symbol of ...
☐ Warmth and holiday cheer
☐ God's presence
☐ Jesus' resurrection
☐ Cosmic power

6 <u>Throughout the Scripture, fire is a symbol of God's presence</u>. God came to Moses in a burning bush (Exodus 3). God led His people through the desert with a pillar of fire that burned in the night (Exodus 13:21). The prophets declared that God's words were like a fire (Jeremiah 23:29). If our God is a "consuming fire" (Hebrews 12:29), then it only makes sense that His Spirit fans the flame of that fire in the heart of every person who truly seeks to follow Him. The entire Book of Acts (and you could argue even the rest of the New Testament) is all about how the Spirit works to overcome obstacles to faith in Jesus. Within just a few decades after the resurrection of Jesus, the church moved from being a few dozen scared and confused followers to become the greatest movement of God the world had ever seen! Where did the power come from for this kind of focus, determination, and resolve? It came from the personal care and awesome fire of the Holy Spirit, which fueled hearts and got the attention of people everywhere.

God is Power

Today is no different. The Holy Spirit helps believers in the same amazing ways, several of which are suggested in this passage. First, **7** <u>the Holy Spirit gives us abilities that we can use to serve God and others</u>. In this passage, the people gathered began to speak in other tongues so that people would hear in their own language that God was up to something. The Spirit today still gives gifts and abilities that will help serve the people of the church and draw people's attention to Him. First Corinthians 12, Romans 12, and Ephesians 4 all discuss how the Spirit empowers people with spiritual gifts for the purpose of building up the other people that form the "body of Christ." Second, **7** <u>the Spirit helps teach us what we need to know</u>. Jesus promised the "counselor" would help teach us and remind us of what He taught at the same time. He also assured that the Spirit would "guide you into all truth" (John 16:12-13). We worship in "spirit and in truth" (John 4:24), and the Spirit guides us in decisions (2 Corinthians 2:10). **7** Finally, <u>the Spirit also brings about unity in the church</u>. He brings Christ-followers together (in spite our differences) to a mutual love, respect, and understanding of one another. Have you ever met another Christ-follower and immediately felt connected like you had been friends forever? That is the Holy Spirit at work (Acts 10:34-35)!

7 In what three ways does the Holy Spirit help us?
1) _____
2) _____
3) _____

12

SMALL-GROUP TIME:
Use this time to help students begin to integrate the truth they've learned into their lives while they connect with the other students in the group, the leaders, and with God.

Ask students to divide back into small groups and discuss the "Do What?" questions. Small-group facilitators should lead the discussions and be sensitive to questions and confusion about the Holy Spirit.

Small-group facilitators should reinforce the LifePoint for this session. Make sure that student's questions are invited and addressed honestly.

 # Do What? *(15 MINUTES)*

Fired Up!

1. How has this week's session given you a better grasp of who the Holy Spirit is and what His desire and role is?

2. In what areas of your life do you feel most in need of connecting with the Holy Spirit? What difference does it make to you to know that He is with you?

3. It's exciting to think that the Holy Spirit is an ever-present help for us. Which of the Holy Spirit's roles most "fires you up" as you think about today's lesson?
   ☐ The power of God (1 Samuel 11:6)
   ☐ The Counselor who brings truth and understanding (John 14:26)
   ☐ The spiritual fuel that powers our mission as believers in life (Acts 4:31)
   ☐ The unifying force that brings followers of Jesus together (Romans 5:5)
   ☐ The giver of gifts for the building up and mission of the church (Romans 12:3)

 # LifePoint Review

The Holy Spirit isn't a mystical force. He is the active third person of the Trinity who gives power and direction to every true Christ-follower and the church.

"Do" Points:

These "Do" Points will help you grab hold of this week's LifePoint. Be open and honest as you answer the questions within your small group.

1. Accept the Holy Spirit as your guide who desperately wants to help you and empower you to live the amazing life God the Father intended for just for you! We must be careful not to neglect the Holy Spirit because He points us toward Jesus. When you need specific guidance or face difficulty, it is biblical and very appropriate to ask the Spirit to lead, guide, comfort, or direct you.
   In what situations might it be best to address the Holy Spirit in prayer? How can you begin incorporating the Spirit into your mindset and prayers?

2. <u>Embrace the unique role in the larger story for which the Holy Spirit has gifted you.</u> It's tempting to sit on our talents and abilities when it comes to church. Natural singers don't want to sing. Born teachers don't want to teach. Some of us think we have nothing to offer, but that's a lie we must not accept.
With what gifts has the Holy Spirit specifically equipped you? How can you use your supernatural gifts, natural talents, and life experiences to help the church and to reach out to people who need Jesus?

3. <u>Develop your gifts through the Holy Spirit's direction and power.</u> Practice makes perfect. And if we neglect to use our gifts and abilities, we'll never know what potential we might have reached with them.
Have you ever sensed the Holy Spirit prodding you to embrace or polish a specific talent? If so, share your story with the group.

Be sure to end your session by asking students to share prayer needs with one another, especially as they relate to issues brought up by today's session.

Encourage students to list prayer needs for others in their books so they can pray for one another during the week. Assign a student coordinator in each small group to gather the group's requests and e-mail them to the group members.

Prayer Connection:

Share prayer needs with the group, especially those related to trusting the Holy Spirit to encourage you in your efforts to live for Jesus and to tell others about Him. Your group facilitator will close your time in prayer.

Prayer Needs:

12

now What?

Encourage students to dig a little deeper by completing a "Now What?" assignment before the next time you meet. Remind students about the "Are You Ready?" short daily Bible readings and related questions at the beginning of Session 13.

Remind them too they are loved and that God the Holy Spirit wants to do amazing things in their lives!

Deepen your understanding of who the Holy Spirit is and continue the journey you've begun today by choosing one of the following assignments to complete this week:

Option #1:

Examine teaching from the Bible of that focuses on spiritual gifts: Ephesians 4, 1 Corinthians 12, and Romans 12. Make a list of specific spiritual gifts and talents you have that could be used to serve the church and people who don't know Jesus.

Option #2:

Research major movements of the Holy Spirit in modern history. The "First Great Awakening" began in New England with the preaching of Jonathan Edwards and George Whitefield in the 1730's. The "Second Great Awakening" (1795-1830) transformed America with its emphasis on social justice and the role of the United States in changing the world. The "Azusa Street Revival" started in Los Angeles in 1906 and began the charismatic church movement. What are characteristics of each of these "revivals?" What similarities do they share with the experience of the early church? How are they different? There are many controversies that surround the movement of the Holy Spirit today. How do we distinguish authentic movements of the Spirit from false teachings and fakes who only claim to be in touch with the Spirit?

Bible Reference notes

Use these notes to deepen your understanding as you study the Bible on your own:

Acts 2:1-13

2:1 the day of Pentecost. This was the Feast of Weeks (Ex. 23:16; Lev. 23:15-21; Deut. 16:9-12) held 50 days after Passover. Originally, a kind of Thanksgiving Day for gathered crops, it came to be associated with the commemoration of the giving of the Law at Sinai (Ex. 20:1-17). Jewish tradition held that when God gave the Law to Moses, a single voice spoke that was heard by all the nations of the world in their own language. Luke may be alluding to that in this story. Pentecost was a celebration to which thousands of Jews from all over the empire would attend.

2:2-4 a violent rushing wind. In both Hebrew (the language in which the Old Testament was originally written) and Greek (the language in which the New Testament was originally written), the word translated as "Spirit" and "wind" and "breath" is all the same word. In Hebrew the word is *rhuah*. In Greek the word is *pneuma*. While this can lead to confusion, it also adds meaning. Is this "wind" from heaven truly a wind or is it the Spirit of God? Actually, it's both! Similarly when God breathed into humankind the "breath" of life (Gen. 2:7), was it really the "breath" of life or the "Spirit" of life? Again, it was both! Note also that it was a violent wind that came at Pentecost. What does that say to us? It reminds us that while the Holy Spirit can bring peace to the soul, the Spirit is also a powerful force that we cannot expect to control or stifle. **like flames of fire.** Fire is often associated with divine appearances (Ex. 3:2; 19:18). John the Baptist said Jesus would baptize his followers with the Holy Spirit and fire (Luke 3:16), symbolizing the cleansing, purifying effect of the Spirit. What is important here is that tongues served as a sign to the crowds of a supernatural event, the point of which was Jesus Christ.

2:9-11 Parthians, Medes, Elamites ... Mesopotamia. Present day Iran and Iraq, to the east of Jerusalem. These Jews traced their roots back to the Assyrian overthrow of Israel and the Babylonian overthrow of Judea seven and five centuries before respectively. **Judea.** Either the immediate environs around Jerusalem are in view, or Luke is referring to the days under David and Solomon when the land of Israel stretched from Egypt on the west to the Euphrates River on the east. **Cappadocia, Pontus and Asia, Phrygia and Pamphylia.** Present day Turkey to the north of Jerusalem. Much of Acts takes place in this region. **Egypt ... Libya near Cyrene.** To the west of Jerusalem on the northern coast of Africa. **proselytes.** Judaism's high morality and developed spirituality attracted many Gentiles from other religions. **Cretans.** An island south of Greece in the Mediterranean Sea. **Arabs.** The Nabetean kingdom was south of Jerusalem with borders on Egypt and the Euphrates.

John 14:26

14:26 the Father will send Him. Here and in verse 16 it is the Father who sends the Spirit to the believe **14:26 the Father will send Him.** Here and in verse 16 it is the Father who sends the Spirit to the believer. In 15:26 and 16:7, Jesus says He will send the Spirit. **will teach you ... remind you.** These parallel verbs are two ways of saying the same thing. The purpose of the teaching of the Spirit is not to impart new information, but to remind believers of the truth Jesus taught and help them apply it to ever-changing situations.

12

NOTES

Session

13

AMAZING: WHAT'S SO IMPORTANT ABOUT GRACE?

Connections Prep

MAIN LIFEPOINT:

We don't deserve it. We can't earn it. That's why grace—God's loving acceptance of us—is truly an amazing gift. It's grace that frees us from bondage and opens the door to new life and eternity. It's grace too that gives us freedom as we learn to walk in that new life with Jesus.

To reinforce the LifePoint, leaders and small-group facilitators should understand the following more detailed CheckPoints and "Do" Points.

BIBLE STUDY CHECKPOINTS:

- Grasp that God's grace gives freedom from past mistakes
- Understand that God's grace can't be earned; it's only available as a free gift
- Recognize that God saves us through grace alone because we can't save ourselves

LIFE CHANGE "DO" POINTS:

- Accept God's grace by receiving Jesus as Savior
- Commit to actively engage with a local church, student ministry, and/or small group
- Commit to follow Jesus and chart a course for ongoing spiritual growth and mission focus

PREPARATION:

☐ Review the *Leader's Book* for this session and prepare your teaching.
☐ Determine how you will subdivide students into small discussion groups.
☐ Recruit mature students or adults as small-group facilitators. Be sure these facilitators plan to attend.

REQUIRED SUPPLIES:

☐ *Essential Truth: Inviting Christ into My Reality* Leader books for each group facilitator
☐ *Essential Truth: Inviting Christ into My Reality* Student books for each student
☐ Pens or pencils for each student
☐ U2's song, "Grace" from their album, "All That You Can't Leave Behind."
☐ CD player

13

 **Get Ready**

Read one of these short Bible passages each day, and spend a few minutes wrapping your brain around grace. Write down anything God reveals to you.

MONDAY

Read Romans 11:2-6
Paul had intense feelings regarding the subject of God's grace. What does he tell us about grace here? Have you ever been a part of a special group of people, like the Honor Society or a ball team, which had special privileges or responsibilities? How did it feel to be chosen to be a part of that group?

TUESDAY

Read 1 Peter 1:13
Peter denied Jesus and yet was given the charge to establish the church. He embraced grace for his salvation and his ongoing life. He knew he couldn't earn his way into relationship with God. What did Peter teach us about how to live?

WEDNESDAY

Read 1 Peter 4:10-11
We can talk the importance of our faith all we want, but the challenge is to daily live as a trophy of God's grace. How can you live in the grace of God?

THURSDAY

Read 2 Corinthians 12:7-10
When we think of God's grace, we often think only in terms of what makes us happy in the moment. What struggle does Paul reveal in this passage? What difficulties has God used in your life?

FRIDAY

Read 1 Timothy 1:12-17

Paul said he was the "worst of all sinners." Why do you think he felt that way? Are there days when you feel you can relate? Spend some time reflecting on this passage. Think about how God's grace to Paul is the same grace extended to you.

SATURDAY

Read Romans 5:15-21

How is God's grace a gift to you? Describe the value and significance of grace. What do we get out of all this grace?

SUNDAY

Read Ephesians 2:1-10

Have you ever had a moment when the world felt new and everything seemed to fall into place? If so, try to describe it. How would it feel to be given a fresh start and put your past behind you?

LARGE-GROUP OPENING:
Get everyone's attention. Make announcements. Open your session with a prayer. Read the LifePoint to the students.

 LifePoint

We don't deserve it. We can't earn it. That's why grace—God's loving acceptance of us—is truly an amazing gift. It's grace that frees us from bondage and opens the door to new life and eternity. It's grace too that gives us freedom as we learn to walk in that new life with Jesus.

13

Say What? *(15 MINUTES)*

Play U2's song, "Grace" for the whole group.

Then, break into
SMALL-GROUP TIME:
Call on the mature student or adult leaders you recruited to facilitate each small group through the "Say What?" segment.

Random Question of the Week:

If the Incredible Hulk and Wonder Woman were to marry, what would their kids look like? What combination of super powers do you think they'd inherit?

Group Experience: Rock and Roll and Grace

Ask everyone to listen carefully to the words of U2's song, "Grace." Play the CD and then instruct students to separate into their small groups.

After you have listened to U2's song, "Grace," discuss the following questions within your small group.

1. What does, "Grace covers the shame, removes the stain" mean in this song? Can you think of a real life example of how this works?

2. The invention of the printing press, Galileo's theory that the earth revolves around the sun, and Newton's work with gravity all radically changed the world. How and why does grace fit under the category "world changing concepts"?

QUESTION 3 NOTE:
We can't earn God's grace; it is freely given instead of something we earn by our own goodness.

3. "Karma" is the Hindu belief that for every good thing we do, something good will happen to us. "What does the songwriter mean when he says, "Grace travels outside of karma"? How does grace "trump" karma in this sense?

Question 4 Note:
Possible responses:
Broken lives are changed; the cross itself was ugly but stands as a symbol of Jesus' beautiful sacrifice to save and restore us to our original glory in Him.

4. Do you agree with this lyric: "Grace makes beauty out of ugly things"? Why or why not? Can you think of examples where this is true?

LARGE-GROUP TIME:
Have the students turn to face the front for this teaching time. Be sure you can make eye contact with each student in the room. Encourage students to follow along and take notes in their *Student Books*.

Share the "So What?" information with your large group of students. You may modify it with your own perspectives and teaching needs. Be sure to highlight the underlined information, which gives answers to the *Student Book* questions and fill-in-the-blanks (shown in your margins).

 # So What? *(30 MINUTES)*

Teaching Outline

I. Grace: Hope for the Undeserving
A. What is grace? Where does it come from? What does it do?

B. *The Ragamuffin Gospel*, (Brennan Manning) - "I am deeply loved by Jesus Christ and I have done nothing to earn it or deserve it."

C. Grace is a gift, freely offered by God to all who accept a relationship with Jesus Christ

D. "Grace" captures heart action of God
  1. He looks beyond our rebellion
  2. He refuses to remember our disobedience and failures anymore
  3. He accepts us as without blame
  4. He forgives us
  5. He adopts us as sons & daughters

E. No one can earn this grace, but everyone desperately longs to be forgiven ... to be clean ... to be accepted in love

II. Ephesians 2:1-10 (NIV)

III. We're Already Dead
A. Nobody's perfect — every person born a liar, a rebel, & a moral failure

B. We want to do things our own way & don't really care what anyone has to say about it

C. Apostle Paul said people are "dead in ... transgressions and sins" (Eph. 2:1-2).
  1. We come into this world as people already dead
  2. We inherited an old nature that is rebellious and sinful
  3. Because of this old nature + our mistakes, shortcomings, & disobedience ... we are hopelessly separated from God

IV. We Need a Rescuer
A. No matter how hard we try, there's just no way we can meet God's standard for perfection

B. We can't restore our relationship with God & regain the original glory He intended for us

13

C. Stuck in an impossible dilemma

D. We need a rescuer, a new nature, a new heart, & a new start

V. Rescued and Restored

A. Since we couldn't get to God on our own efforts, He came to us!

B. Ephesians 2:4-5 provides God's solution to humanity's biggest problem

    1. God extended grace to us by sending Jesus

    2. Jesus, the perfect God-man died to pay for every wrong we ever have or ever will do

C. What we need to do to reach God

    1. Ask for His forgiveness

    2. Accept, through faith in Jesus and His sacrifice for us

    3. Embrace the free gift of a new nature, a new heart, & the promise of eternity

VI. Life Nobody Can Buy

A. Most would pay any amount to be truly free from our past

B. But we can never pay or do enough to earn God's that freedom and a new start; it's only available as a gift: "For it is by grace you have been saved through faith ... not by works, so that no one can boast" (Eph. 3:8-9).

C. Jesus provides hope and freedom, but requires our faith and total dependence on Him

D. When Jesus saves and transforms us—as we trust fully in Him we find:

    1. Healing, freedom, peace, and joy as our past, present, and future

    2. Forgiveness

    3. Restored relationship with God

    4. Freedom & joy in joining God in His mission of healing & restoring of people

    5. A future with anticipation of paradise & eternity with God

TEACHING FOR THE LARGE GROUP: Share the "So What?" teaching with your students. You may modify it to fit your needs.

Be sure to highlight the underlined information, which gives answers to the *Student Book* questions and fill-in-the-blanks (shown in your margins)

1 Brennan Manning summarizes _grace_ as we know it when he writes, "I am deeply _loved_ by Jesus Christ and I have done nothing to _earn_ it or _deserve_ it."

2 What four actions of God does the term "grace" capture?

1) _____

2) _____

3) _____

4) _____

3 Why is "Amazing Grace" one of the most famous hymns in the world?

Learning from the Bible ...

Ephesians 2:1-10 NIV

You may read the passage yourself or ask a volunteer to come to the front of the room and read it.

Grace: Hope for the Undeserving

What is grace? Where does it come from? What does it do? In his book, *The Ragamuffin Gospel*, author **1** Brennan Manning summarizes grace as we know it: "I am deeply loved by Jesus Christ and I have done nothing to earn it or deserve it." Grace is a gift, freely offered by God to all who accept a relationship with Jesus Christ. **2** The term captures the heart and action of God in which—because of His amazing love—He looks beyond our rebellion, refuses to remember it anymore, accepts us as without blame, forgives us, and adopts us as sons and daughters. Too often we try to earn God's acceptance by trying hard to be good enough or pushing ourselves to live by a rigid set of rules. No one can earn this grace, but everyone desperately needs it.

3 "Amazing Grace" is the most famous hymn in the world for a reason. People have a desperate inner longing to be forgiven ... to be clean ... to be accepted in love. Today as we wrap up this study on inviting Christ into our reality, we're going to look at how grace works and how it impacts the lives of individual believers.

Learning from the Bible

1 As for you, you were dead in your transgressions and sins, 2 in which you used to live when you followed the ways of this world and the ruler of the kingdom of the air, the spirit who is now at work in those who are disobedient. 3 All of us who lived among them at one time, gratifying the cravings of our sinful nature and following its desires and thoughts. Like the rest, we were by nature objects of wrath. 4 But because of his great love for us, God, who is rich in mercy, 5 made us alive with Christ even when we were dead in transgressions—it is by grace you have been saved. 6 And God raised us up with Christ and seated us with Him in the heavenly realms in Christ Jesus, 7 in order that in the coming ages he might show the incomparable riches of His grace, expressed in his] kindness to us in Christ Jesus. 8 For it is by grace you have been saved through faith—and this not from yourselves, it is the gift of God— 9 not by works, so that no one can boast. 10 For we are God's workmanship, created in Christ Jesus to do good works, which God prepared in advance for us to do.

LARGE-GROUP TIME CONTINUED: This is the meat of the teaching time. Remind students to follow along and take notes in their *Student Books.*

We're Already Dead

Nobody's perfect. In fact, every person is born a liar, a rebel, and a moral failure. From the moment we understand the meaning of "no," we fight it. We want to do things our own way, and by nature we don't really care what anyone has to say about it. No matter how hard we try, we do things that keep us from God and even

13

from other people. We're stubborn, self-centered, and prone to wander through life with a chip on our shoulders. ❹ <u>The Apostle Paul summed up the human condition this way: people are "dead in ... transgressions and sins" (verses 1-2). In other words, we come into this world as people already dead because we inherited an old nature that is rebellious and sinful. Because of this old nature as well as our mistakes, shortcomings, and disobedience that come out of that nature, we are hopelessly separated from God.</u>

❹ What is the Apostle Paul referring to in saying that people are "dead" in "transgressions (wrongdoings, offenses) and sins (rebellion, disobedience)"?

We Need a Rescuer

No matter how hard we try, there's just no way we can meet the standard for perfection needed to restore our relationship with God and the original glory He intended for us. This leaves us stuck in an impossible dilemma. ❺ <u>We need a rescuer, a new nature, a new heart, and a new start. Since we couldn't get to God on our own efforts, He came to us!</u>

❺ We need a *rescuer*, a new *nature*, a new *heart*, and a new *start*. Since we couldn't get to God on our own efforts, *He came to us*!

Rescued and Restored

Ephesians 2:4-5 provides God's solution to humanity's biggest problem: But because of his great love for us, God, who is rich in mercy, made us alive with Christ even when we were dead in transgressions—it is by grace you have been saved." In other words, ❻ <u>God extended grace to us by sending Jesus, the perfect God-man to die in payment for everything we ever have or ever will do wrong. All we need to do now to reach God is ask for His forgiveness and accept, through faith in Jesus and His sacrifice for us, the free gift of a new nature, a new heart, and the promise of eternity.</u>

❻ How did God provide a solution to our impossible dilemma? What do we have to do escape our dilemma?

Most of us would pay any amount of money to be truly free from our past. *But we can never pay or do enough to earn God's that freedom and a new start; it's only available as a gift: "For it is by grace you have been saved through faith ... not by works, so that no one can boast." ❼ This beautiful fact provides hope and freedom, but it requires our faith and total dependence on Jesus who alone is able to save and transform our lives. It ❽ <u>And when Jesus saves and transforms us, and we trust fully in Him, we find healing, freedom, peace, and joy as our past, present, and future are forgiven and our relationship with God is restored. In our joy and freedom, we can join God in His mission of healing and restoring of people. We can also turn to the future with anticipation of paradise and eternity with God.</u>

❼ Grace is a gift that we must earn. *True* or *False*

❽ After we are saved "by grace" what begins to happen in and through our lives?

SMALL-GROUP TIME:
Use this time to help students begin to integrate the truth they've learned into their lives while they connect with the other students in the group, the leaders, and with God.

Ask students to divide back into small groups and discuss the "Do What?" questions.

Do What? *(15 MINUTES)*

Bringing Grace Home

1. Do you feel like you understand grace better? Let's see what unique perspectives each of us might bring. Put the idea of "grace" in your own words.

2. If it's true what people say—that nothing we can do will make God love us any less—then what's the point of making positive decisions in how we live our lives?

3. To what degree do you feel like you have "gotten what you deserve" in life?
   - ☐ I deserve better – I always get short changed!
   - ☐ I deserve what I want – I've earned the right to live life my way.
   - ☐ I deserve what I've gotten – I'm living with the consequences of my mistakes.
   - ☐ I deserve much less – God has been good to me.
   - ☐ Other: _____

QUESTION 4 NOTE:
Remind students about previous discussions in this session that highlight ineffective ways to gain eternal life.

Be sensitive to those who are ready to make a new or deeper commitment to Jesus; invite students who'd like to talk further about eternal life to stay after the session.

4. If you had to stand before God today and tell Him why you deserved to get into heaven, what would you say?
   - ☐ I'm basically a good person.
   - ☐ I'm better than most people.
   - ☐ I help others.
   - ☐ I attend church.
   - ☐ I accepted Jesus' offer of forgiveness and a new life.
   - ☐ Other: _____

5. If you have chosen to accept God's gift of grace, in what ways has it changed your life?

13

LifePoint Review

We don't deserve it. We can't earn it. That's why grace—God's loving acceptance of us—is truly an amazing gift. It's grace that frees us from bondage and opens the door to new life and eternity. It's grace too that gives us freedom as we learn to walk in that new life with Jesus.

"Do" Points:

These "Do" Points will help you grab hold of this week's LifePoint. Be open and honest as you answer the questions within your small group.

1. <u>Accept God's grace by receiving Jesus as Savior.</u> Salvation is a free gift, but you must accept it. God won't force it on you. He won't take away your freedom to choose because without freedom there is no real love.
   Evaluate your personal commitment to faith in Jesus. If you haven't yet accepted the gift of forgiveness and new life, share with the group what's holding you back. If you have, explain why you did.
   (If you have questions about how to start or deepen your relationship with Jesus, please stay and talk to your small-group leader or student minister about it. They'll be pleased to help you in your journey!)

2. <u>Commit to actively engage with a local church, student ministry, and/or small group.</u> Being part of a church is a vital decision for your continued growth and your effectiveness in furthering God's mission of bringing hope, freedom, and life to people trapped in darkness. Engaging in a church says you will worship, grow, and serve with a local group of Jesus-followers who are committed to each other and to making a difference in the world for God.
   What steps can you take to more actively connect with other Christ-followers? Why is it so important that you do? What might happen if you don't?

3. <u>Commit to follow Jesus and chart a course for ongoing spiritual growth and mission focus.</u> God won't allow those committed to a relationship with Him to stay complacent. He wants us to grow in our connection with Him and to constantly learn more about Him and His ways.
   How can you move forward in your spiritual journey? What attitudes, behaviors, and habits do you think indicate a commitment to spiritual growth?

Be sure to end your session by asking students to share prayer needs with one another, especially as they relate to issues brought up by today's session.

Encourage students to list prayer needs for others in their books so they can pray for one another during the week. Assign a student coordinator in each small group to gather the group's requests and e-mail them to the group members.

Encourage students to dig a little deeper by completing a "Now What" assignment even though this study is complete.

Encourage them to accept God's grace and to continue to live in that grace!

Prayer Connection:

Share prayer needs with the group, especially those related to accepting God's forgiveness and accepting His offer of relationship with Him. Your group facilitator will close your time in prayer.

Prayer Needs:

Deepen your understanding of what grace truly means to us, and continue the journey you've begun today by choosing one of the following assignments to complete this week:

Option #1:

Become an agent of grace. If someone hurts you this week, write that person a note offering your forgiveness—whether or not you feel it's deserved. Remember, God freely forgives you. Be quick to forgive others.

Option #2:

Stay in touch with those in your small group. Keep a running thread of discussion going about how you're experiencing God's grace each week.

Option #3:

Contact a local ministry or church that reaches out to prisoners. Work with a prison chaplain to get a list of men and women to whom you can write. Encourage them with your own story of grace. Share God's personal offer of grace with them. (Caution: Be careful not to provide personal information in your correspondence. Work with the prison chaplain about precautions you should take.)

13

Bible Reference notes

Use these notes to deepen your understanding as you study the Bible on your own:

Ephesians 2:1-10

2:1 dead. They were spiritually dead. ***transgressions and sins.*** These two words refer, respectively, to active wrongdoing ("sins of commission"), and passive failure ("sins of omission").

2:2 ruler of the kingdom of the air. This is the first of several references in Ephesians to Satan, the Devil. ***now at work.*** Satan's activity is not only past, nor only in the future. It is here and now in this present evil age. ***those who are disobedient.*** They are, in fact, in active rebellion against God.

2:3 our sinful nature. The word here is literally "the flesh," and it refers to self-centered human nature that expresses itself in destructive activities of both body and mind.

2:4 abundant. Paul makes more allusions to "riches" in Ephesians than anywhere else in his writings. ***mercy.*** Not only love, but also mercy motivates God. Love and mercy are closely related. ***because of His great love.*** Love is God's reason for rescuing fallen humanity (Deut. 7:6-9This is one of four words that Paul uses to explain God's motivation for reaching out to humanity: love, mercy, grace, and kindness.

2:5 made us alive. Paul coins this word to describe exactly what happens to us when we are "in Christ;" namely, we share in Christ's resurrection, ascension, and enthronement. ***by grace.*** This resurrection from spiritual death cannot be earned. It is simply given. Grace is God's unmerited favor or gift to us. We can't earn it and don't deserve it, but God offers it because of His amazing love.

2:8 For it is by grace you have been saved. This is the second time Paul acclaims this amazing fact (v. 5). ***through faith.*** Salvation does not come about because of faith. Salvation comes by grace (from God) through faith (from us).

2:8–9 not from yourselves ... not by works. Salvation is not a reward for being good or keeping the Law.

2:10 good works. Although good works do not save a person, they are a result of salvation.

Romans 5:15-21

5:15 gift. This could refer Christ and His work on behalf of humanity, but in light of verses 18, 20, and 21, it probably indicates the status conferred on humanity of being counted righteous before God.

5:16 from one sin came the judgment ... justification. One act of disobedience by Adam brought judgment and condemnation to all, but Christ's gift brings justification and forgiveness not only for that one sin, but also for all the sins down through the centuries.

5:18-19 one man's disobedience ... one man's obedience. With the dissimilarity between Adam and Christ established, Paul can return to the formal comparison he began in verse 12: One man's disobedience brought condemnation and death to all, just as one man's obedience now brings justification and life to all who choose it. The only similarity between Christ and Adam is that by a single deed each had an incalculable impact on all of humanity.

5:18 one righteous act. The obedience of Christ's whole life, which led to His sacrificial death.

5:20 law. When the law came, it served to define what was in fact "sinful"—it brought "sin" into clear view by functioning as a mirror.

Acknowledgments:

We sincerely appreciate the great team of people that worked to develop this study on *Essential Truth, Youth Edition.* Special thanks are extended to Jay Strother for writing this study. We also appreciate the editorial and production team that consisted of Ben Colter, Scott Lee, Joe Moore of Powell Creative, Bethany McShurley, and Sarah Hogg.

NOTES

PASS THIS DIRECTORY AROUND AND HAVE YOUR GROUP
MEMBERS FILL IN THEIR NAMES AND PHONE NUMBERS.

NAME	PHONE	E-MAIL